# OMAN

# PROFILES · NATIONS OF THE CONTEMPORARY MIDDLE EAST
Bernard Reich and David E. Long,
Series Editors

# ABOUT THE BOOK AND AUTHOR

Until the 1970s Oman was an isolated, almost medieval kingdom, virtually unknown to the outside world. The 1970 palace coup that brought Sultan Qaboos b. Sa'id Al-Sa'id to power also brought Oman into the twentieth century. Development programs made modernization a rapid process, and Oman's location at the entrance to the Straits of Hormuz gave the country an increasing importance to U.S. security interests in the Gulf region.

Yet despite modernization, Oman remains an unknown land. In this book, Calvin H. Allen, Jr., dispels some of the mystery by focusing on the land, the people, and the history of this Middle Eastern nation. Dr. Allen explores the influences on events of trade, foreign involvement in Omani affairs, and Ibadism (the principal sect of Islam in Oman). He also emphasizes the role Qaboos b. Sa'id Al-Sa'id has played in contemporary Oman. The architect of Oman's "new age," Qaboos has overseen significant changes in the country's political system, rapid economic growth financed by oil exports, and increased Omani participation in world affairs. In looking at the sultanate from a broad perspective, the author provides a panoramic view of a nation emerging from obscurity to take its place in the modern world.

Calvin H. Allen, Jr., is associate professor of history at The School of the Ozarks in Missouri.

# OMAN

## The Modernization
## of the Sultanate

Calvin H. Allen, Jr.

Westview Press • Boulder, Colorado

Croom Helm • London and Sydney

*Profiles/Nations of the Contemporary Middle East*

Copyright © 1987 by Westview Press, Inc.

Published in 1987 in the United States of America by Westview Press, Inc.; Frederick A. Praeger, Publisher; 5500 Central Avenue, Boulder, Colorado 80301

Published in 1987 in Great Britain by Croom Helm Ltd., Provident House, Burrell Row, Beckenham, Kent, BR3 1AT

Library of Congress Cataloging-in-Publication Data
Allen, Calvin H., Jr.
  Oman: the modernization of the sultanate.
  (Profiles. Nations of the contemporary Middle East)
  Bibliography: p.
  Includes index.
  1. Oman.  I. Title.  II. Series.
DS247.06A75  1986     953′.53     86-15806
ISBN 0-8133-0125-4 (alk. paper)

British Library Cataloguing-in-Publication Data
Allen, Calvin H., Jr.
  Oman: the modernization of the sultanate.
  (Profiles: nations of the contemporary Middle East)
  1. Oman—History
  I. Title  II. Series
  953′.53     DS247.065
ISBN 0-7099-5106-X

Printed and bound in the United States of America

The paper used in this publication meets the requirements of the American National Standard for Permanence of Paper for Printed Library Materials Z39.48-1984.

10   9   8   7   6   5   4   3   2   1

# Contents

vii

# Illustrations

# *Preface*

Oman, formerly known as Muscat and Oman, is one of the few places left in the world that still inspires interest because of its isolation and mystery. My own interest in Arabia and in Oman in particular began when I was a teenager in the early 1960s when stamps from obscure places like Abu Dhabi, Dubai, Umm al-Qiwain, Ras al-Khaima, Qatar, and Muscat and Oman, depicting the bearded visages of Arab shaiks and beau geste forts began appearing in my collection. My interest piqued, I began searching for information on these people and places. I could find little, especially on Oman, which was still closed to almost all outsiders by Sultan Sa'id b. Taimur. By the late 1960s, however, Oman began to be the focus of scholarly interest: The pioneering works of Wendel Phillips, B. C. Busch, Robert Landen, and J. B. Kelly were published, and reprints of classics by S. B. Miles and P. Badger were issued. But contemporary Oman remained veiled.

After the palace coup of 1970 and the coming to power of Sultan Qaboos b. Sa'id, Oman began to emerge from the dark ages. The development programs of the early 1970s brought many foreigners to Oman, and for the first time conducting research within the country became possible. I was fortunate to be one of the first U.S. scholars to spend an extended time there; in 1976–1977, under the sponsorship of Sayyid Faisal b. Ali Al-Sa'id and the newly formed ministry of national heritage and with funding from the Fulbright program, I conducted research on nineteenth-century trade and politics in Muscat. I was able to return to Muscat for a short visit in March–April 1985, thanks to my friends Ranchordas and Vimal Purecha of Ratansi Purshottam Company and grants from the faculty development committee and professional travel fund of The School of the Ozarks. The National Endowment for the Humanities also provided me with money for research on early twentieth-century Oman at the India Office Library and Records in London.

Since 1970 Oman has been the subject of many scholarly books and articles covering various aspects of its history, society, economy, and politics. No single-volume general survey has yet been attempted, though. This book seeks to fill that void. Of necessity, I have drawn upon the works of many others, and to them I express a debt of gratitude. All of these works are described in the bibliographic essay at the end of the book.

I also wish to acknowledge the individual assistance of several teachers, colleagues, and friends who helped to make this book possible. These include my mentors at the University of Washington, Professors Jere Bacharach, Farhat Ziadeh, and Frank Conlon; my colleagues in the history department at The School of the Ozarks, Professors Jim Zabel and Steve Kneeshaw; the floor staff at the India Office for their efficient and courteous service during my two visits there; Mike Gibson of The School of the Ozarks Press for preparing the maps; Dr. Robert W. Stookey of the University of Texas at Austin; Dr. John Wilkinson of Oxford; my parents, Calvin H. and Helen M. Allen; my in-laws, Roger K. and Jeannette W. Strong; and my two sons, Matthew and Drew. Finally, I could never have written this book without the active support of my wife, Becky, who, during the past fifteen years, has managed domestic affairs, served as financier, secretary, sounding board, and morale booster, and performed a host of other tasks well beyond the call of duty. This book is dedicated to her.

*Calvin H. Allen, Jr.*

# Notes to the Reader

1. Transliteration of Arabic words and names has generally followed the system used by the Middle East Studies Association as described in the *International Journal of Middle Eastern Studies.*

2. Throughout the text the term *the Gulf* has been used in place of the Arabian/Persian Gulf.

3. All photos in the book were taken by the author.

C.H.A.

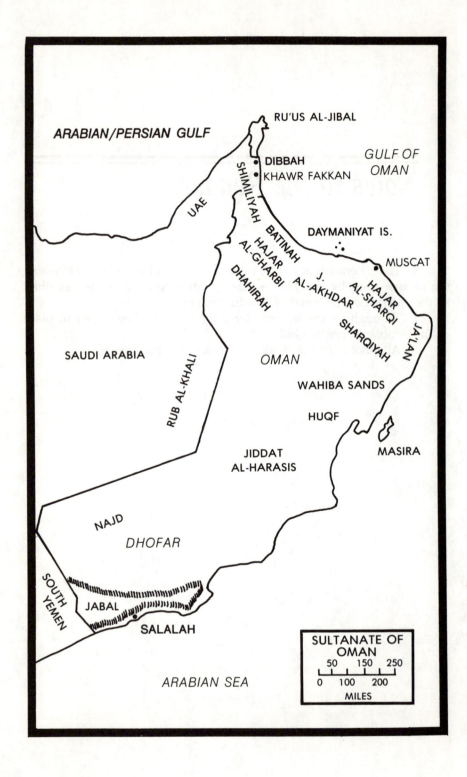

# 1

## Land and People

The country of Oman, situated in the southeastern quarter of the Arabian Peninsula, has a topography, social composition, and traditional economic pattern very typical of the Middle East. The country is virtually cut off from the rest of the peninsula by the Rub al-Khali desert, and its topography is dominated by mountains. Its rough terrain and hot, dry climate, like those of the rest of the peninsula, are not well suited to a settled population; yet for thousands of years the majority of the people have tapped the land's meager water resources and practiced agriculture. Others have turned to the sea to earn a living either as fishermen or as merchants. International trade has meant that Oman has had many overseas contacts with the Indian subcontinent, Africa, and even China. These contacts have had great influence on the country's predominately Arab Muslim population, which has a tribal social organization remarkably divided along religious and ethnic lines.

### THE LAND

The Sultanate of Oman claims a land area of 82,030 square miles (212,460 sq km; roughly the size of Kansas) bordering on South Yemen, Saudi Arabia, and the United Arab Emirates (UAE) as well as the Persian/Arabian Gulf (hereafter referred to as "the Gulf"), the Gulf of Oman, and Arabian Sea. The country is divided into three main regions: Oman, Dhofar, and the exclave of Ru'us al-Jibal.

#### Oman

By far the largest, most heavily populated, and economically important region in the sultanate is Oman. This region, which has given its name to the entire country, stretches from the Gulf of Oman to the sandy wastes of the Rub al-Khali and from the UAE to the Jiddat al-Harasis. At its center are the populated areas around the Hajar Mountains, which run north to southeast in an arc from Dibba on the Shimiliyah

1

coast to Ras al-Hadd. Oman is divided into several subregions including the Batinah coastal plain, the Western Hajar, also known as Oman Proper, the Eastern Hajar, the Capital Area, and Masira Island.

The Batinah is a 150-mile-long (240 km), narrow, low, sandy coastal plain beginning near Liwa in the north and extending to about Sib in the southeast and slowly rising inland for between 10 and 50 miles (16 to 80 km) to piedmont before reaching the Hajar Mountains. The plain is transversed by a series of wadis (dry river beds) formed by runoff from the mountains. The climate is hot and dry, although it is somewhat moderated by sea breezes along the coast, and receives only about 4 inches of rain per year, mostly in July, at the beginning of the monsoon, and in December. Natural vegetation includes some wild grasses, thorny shrubs, and the deep-rooted acacia tree. This is Oman's most densely populated area, consisting of a band of major port towns like Sohar, Khabura, Suwayq, Masna'a, Birka, and Sib and large agricultural settlements extending down the coast and inland for 1 mile (1.6 km). The Batinah also includes the uninhabited Daymaniyat Islands near Birka.

Inland from the Batinah is the Western Hajar region, also known as Oman Proper. This is the core area of Oman: the first area settled in ancient times and throughout history the area providing the focus for Omani culture. Centered on the massive Jabal al-Akhdar, actually a high (10,000 feet; 3,000 m) plateau, the Western Hajar includes several knots of settlements around the base of the mountain. On the eastern side is the Ghadaf with the towns of Rustaq, Awabi, Iffi, and Nakhl. Beginning in the north, the western side of the Jabal has the settlements of Tu'am, around the Buraimi Oasis, Sirr, including the towns of Dhank, Yanqul, and Ibri, and the Jawf, with Nizwa, Bahla, Izki, and Manah. These highly populated areas nestled in the foothills give way to the Dhahirah, an uneven, gravelly, barren, lightly populated plain that disappears into the Rub al-Khali.

Western Hajar's terrain is rugged, almost lunar in its appearance. The limestone and dolomite mountains have been sharply etched, and the entire region is incised by wadis. The latter have played a very important role in the area not only as a source of water but also in facilitating communication both internally and with other regions. Three of these wadis, al-Jizzi in the north, Hawasina in the center, and the Sama'il gap in the south, have ensured that the interior and coast were closely linked. The climate of the Western Hajar differs little from that of the Batinah. The mountains result in higher average rainfall of 10 inches (25 cm), and temperatures are also higher. Natural vegetation is limited to some grasses, shrubs, and acacias and becomes progressively sparser as one moves away from the mountains.

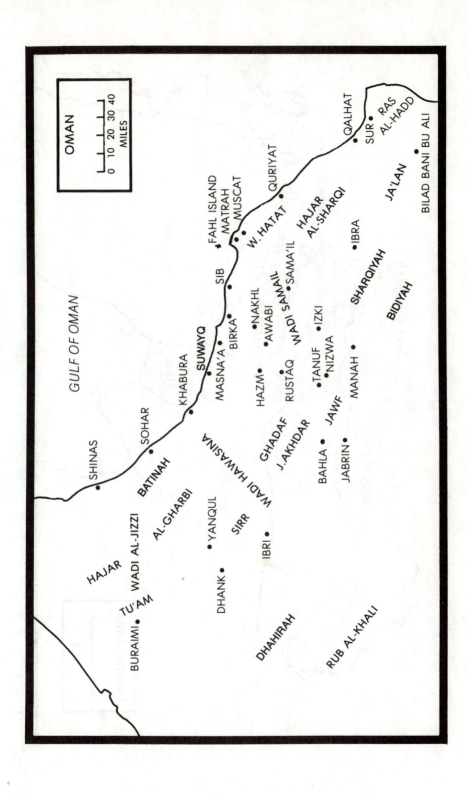

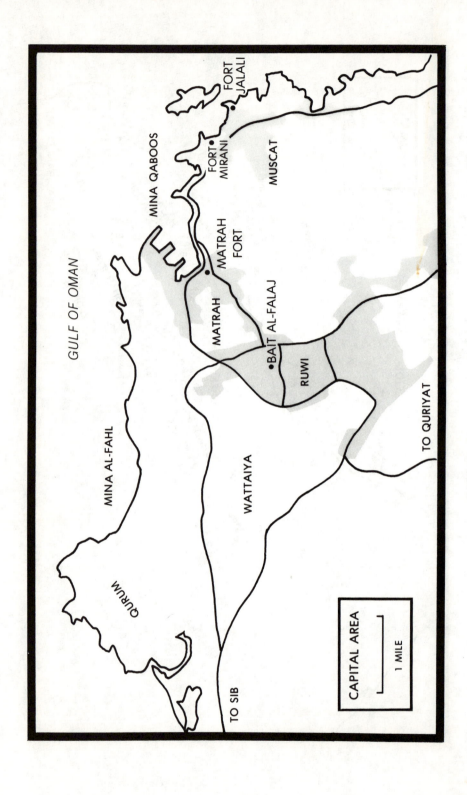

Eastern Hajar is divided from the west by the Sama'il gap and is more rugged and lightly populated than the western mountains. The main settlement area is the Sharqiyah, which includes the towns of Samad and Ibra; the more lightly populated Bidiyah and Ja'lan subregions extend to the south and west before the Western Hajar ends at the Wahiba sands, the Huqf, the Jiddat al-Harasis, and the Rub al-Khali. Topography, climate, and vegetation are the same as those in the Western Hajar. The region is served by the port of Sur.

Although technically located in the Eastern Hajar, for political, cultural, and economic reasons the Capital Area, extending from Sib to Quriyat and including the metropolitan area of Muscat-Mutrah-Ruwi and al-Fahl Island, is considered a separate subregion. The Capital Area is situated at the southeastern extremity of the Hajar Mountains where they plunge into the sea forming a number of fine, albeit small, natural harbors. The mountains have also served to isolate the Capital Area from the rest of Oman. In modern times Muscat and Matrah became the centers of commerce for Oman and attracted a large resident foreign population. Today they also serve as administrative and industrial centers and receive an overwhelmingly disproportionate share of government and private investment in development, which further differentiates them from the rest of Oman.

Masira if the largest and most important island possession of the sultanate. It lies off the barren coast of the Huqf and is 40 miles (64 km) long by about 10 miles (16 km) wide. The island is hilly with little natural vegetation and sparsely populated, with its inhabitants engaged almost entirely in fishing.

### Dhofar

Dhofar, bordering on the Hadramaut region of South Yemen, the Rub al-Khali, and the sparsely populated Huqf and Jiddat al-Harasis areas, is the sultanate's second main region. Dhofar, like Oman, has a narrow coastal plain, known as the Salalah Plain or the Jurbaib, which extends about 30 miles (48 km) from Mirbat to Rakhyut and inland for about 10 miles (16 km). Several wadis, some ending in small creeks, cross the plain providing moisture for grasses. The climate is more moderate than that of the north, and Salalah receives about 6 inches (15 cm) of rain a year, all during the monsoon of July and August. The Salalah Plain is the most densely populated area in Dhofar, and most of its people live in Salalah, the sultanate's largest city, with an estimated 30,000 people.

Inland from the Salalah Plain are three mountain blocks: from west to east, Jabal Qamar, Jabal Qara, and Jabal Samhan. The southern exposures of these mountains receive approximately 30 inches (75 cm)

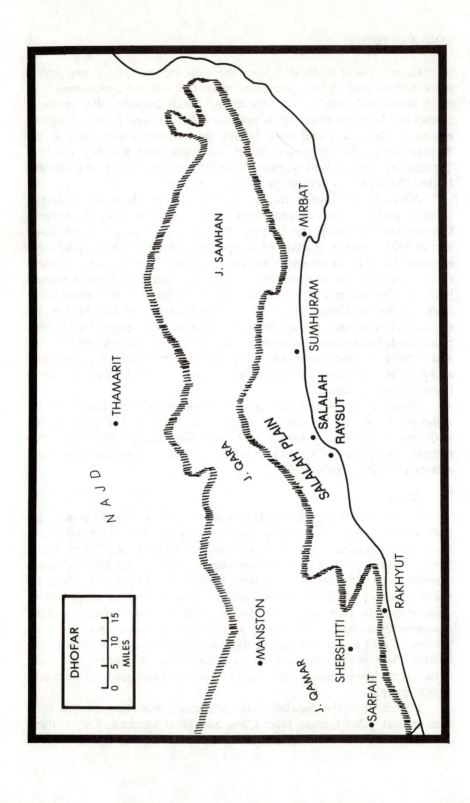

DHOFAR

0  5  10  15
MILES

THAMARIT

NAJD

J. GARA

J. SAMHAN

SALALAH PLAIN

MIRBAT

SUMHURAM

SALALAH

RAYSUT

MANSTON

J. QAMAR

SHERSHITTI

SARFAIT

RAKHYUT

of rain a year, again during the monsoon when the mountains are in
the cloud belt, and this precipitation is sufficient for luxuriant grasslands
and stands of trees unique in Arabia. Although the northern slopes fall
within the rain shadow, they do receive some rainfall. Also on the
northern slopes the frankincense tree for which Dhofar is famous is
found. Beyond the mountains is a gravelly plateau known as the Najd,
which divides the mountains from the desert. Dhofar also includes the
Kuria Muria Islands.

### Ru'us al-Jibal

The final region of the Sultanate is the northern exclave of Ru'us
al-Jibal, also known as the Masandam Peninsula. Ru'us al-Jibal is a
mountainous promontory extending from Bayah, on the Gulf of Oman,
north into the Straits of Hormuz, and then south to Sh'am on the Gulf
and is divided from Oman by the UAE. The northern extension of Ru'us
al-Jibal, the Masandam Peninsula Proper, is separated off by the Ghubbat
al-Ghazira (Malcolm Inlet) and Khawr al-Sham (Elphinstone Inlet) with
the narrow Maqlab Isthmus between them. All the terrain of Ru'us al-
Jibal is rugged mountains extending right to the coast with precipitous
overhanging cliffs and only small bays at the mouths of drowned valleys.
All the main settlements, including Limah, Kumzar, Bukha, and Khasab,
are located on *sails* or outwash fans at the mouths of wadis running
into the sea. Rainfall is negligible, and natural vegetation, save for the
omnipresent acacia, is almost nonexistent. Several uninhabited islands
of strategic importance are located at the northern end of Ru'us al-Jibal
in the Straits of Hormuz. These include Ghanam (Goat) Island, Masandam
Island, and Salamat wa Banatha (the Quoins). The main shipping route
in the straits passes through the 6-mile-wide channel between the last
and the Omani mainland.

### SOCIETY AND CULTURE

For a country with an estimated 1 million people, Oman exhibits
an incredible ethnic diversity. Although Arabs dominate numerically and
culturally, minority groups have flourished, from the Shihuh in Ru'us
al-Jibal, to Indians and Baluchis in Muscat, to Jibalis in Dhofar. Furthermore, the Arab population itself is not homogeneous but is divided
by religious and tribal distinctions.

### Tribal Organization

Oman is an Arab state in which traditional Arab tribal organization
serves as the basis of society. Oman's Arab population is divided into
hundreds of tribes of varying size and cohesiveness with such factors

as genealogical origins, traditional alliances, religion, and economic patterns (settled versus nomadic), all contributing to intertribal solidarity or division. In Oman the tribe has regulated social, territorial, economic, and political relationships.

A tribe is simply a clan or group of clans that is usually organized around a common ancestor, although there is no formal determinant of whom that ancestor must be and it is not even completely necessary that a common ancestor be recognized. In practice all members simply agree that they are a tribe and have obligations to one another. The tribe is a pragmatic institution that can lead to either divisiveness, with tribes claiming only a few members, or unity, with others counting several thousand followers. Tribes can become fragmented and can split into two or more when there is a loss of consensus about an ancestor, as was the case with the Na'im and Al Bu Shamis in the nineteenth century. Conversely, two or more tribes may join together to form a single tribe, as in the Al-Khalili tribal affiliation with the Bani Ruwaha.

Omani tribes have historically had a great deal of local autonomy. All have a formal structure led by a shaikh (sheikh) whose chief duties are to mediate disputes within the group and to lead it when conflict arises with outsiders. The office is not strictly hereditary, but shaikhs are normally selected from an elite family within the tribe. That family's choice is then presented to the other members of the tribe for acceptance. Consensus rather than formal election is the rule. Legitimacy is conferred through continued satisfaction with the manner in which duties are performed.

Tribes with many clans or tribes especially important politically usually have a paramount shaikh, known as *tamimah*. The duties of the tamimah are roughly those of the shaikh, and the selection process is the same, although in practice the position of tamimah is hereditary. Tamimahs have always tended to be involved with "national" affairs rather than purely tribal ones, leaving those to the shaikhs of the individual clans. Five tamimahs, in particular, the Hirth, Bani Riyam (from the Nabahina family), the Bani Ruwaha (from the Al-Khalili), the Hinawi, and the Al Bu Sa'id (from the Al-Sa'id), are most important and have dominated Omani politics for the past two hundred years.

### The Imamate

In addition to this tribal structure, the Arabs have also contributed Oman's dominant religious belief, Islam. Omani Islam is distinct in that it is primarily Ibadism, a branch of the Kharijite schism that broke with orthodoxy during the sixth century over the question of leadership within the Muslim community. For Ibadis, eligibility to be the leader, which they call the imam, is based on merit alone and does not require membership in Muhammad's tribe (the Sunni view) or his immediate family (the Shi'a view).

Ibadism, which takes its name from Abdallah b. Ibad, one of the sects founders, developed in Basra where it was organized by Jabir b. Zaid, a native of Firq (near Nizwa). Differing from more radical Kharijite groups over the question of the proper relationship with non-Kharijites (Ibadis do not believe that these people can be killed legally, and they allow intermarriage), the Ibadis were able to live in relative peace under the early Umayyad Caliphate. During the governorship of al-Hajjaj, however, the group was persecuted, and many of its leaders were imprisoned or, like Jabir b. Zaid, sent into exile in Oman. After the death of al-Hajjaj Ibadism experienced a renaissance in Basra and began sending out missionaries both to spread the religion and to promote revolution for the establishment of an ideal state under a properly elected imam. Converts were gained in North Africa in Algeria and Tunisia and eastern Iran, but the movement met with its greatest success in Oman and actually began electing imams.

The imamate is based on the theory, established at the death of Muhammad, that the Muslim community selects the man that the members of the community consider best able to serve as their leader. Any mature adult male possessing all physical and mental capabilities who is religiously knowledgeable can be considered for the office. Birth gives no special advantage; eligibility must be earned through study. Authority is based on the acceptance and continued satisfaction of the community that the imam is doing a proper job. If the community is no longer satisfied with the imam's performance, authority is lost, and the imam can be deposed. However, revolt against a just imam is considered the worst of crimes. There is also some question as to whether an imam is requisite. The Ibadis believe in the practice of *kitman* (secrecy) when political conditions might require that the existence of an imam be concealed.

The selection process of the imam is not clearly described and has been the cause for much dispute within the sect. The preferred method is election, although even the electing body is poorly defined. By tradition in Oman, the main tribal and religious leaders serve as an electoral college with their candidate presented to the general public, which theoretically has a veto over the choice. Major debates have occurred, sometimes resulting in civil wars, throughout Omani history over the appropriateness of electors. Ibadi theory also makes provision for the acceptance of a leader as an imam without formal election. If the community is satisfied that a ruler is just, no further action is necessary. The imam's authority is recognized simply by the possession of that authority.

Imams combine political and religious functions; there is no separation of church and state. The imam is responsible for the supervision of the tax collections and the distribution of state revenues, and he appoints governors and *qadis* (judges), enforces the *sharia* (Muslim law), provides for the social welfare of the people, and organizes and commands the army. The imam's powers are not absolute though because one of the Ibadi community's greatest fears is tyranny and authoritarian rule. All functions are derived from the sharia, and the imam has no legislative power. Furthermore, the imam is expected to confer with the *ulema* (religious scholars) and general public on matters of general welfare. There is also no standing army. In time of military need, the community is obligated to protect itself or to conduct holy war against unbelievers.

### Confederations

Although Ibadism has historically served as the focus of Omani nationalism, as will be seen in the chapters on history, not all Omani Arabs are Ibadis and the population is also divided between two large tribal confederations—the Hinawi and the Ghafiri. These confederations originated, according to custom, with the southern and northern Arab tribes of antiquity, although the dichotomy probably derives from the Arab settlement of Oman with one faction representing the earlier wave of immigrants and the other the later wave. Whatever the origins, the division was reinforced during a civil war in the ninth century when the southern Arabs, the earlier settlers, now known as the Yaman, supported one imam and the northern Arabs, known as the Nizar, supported another. In a second civil war in the eighteenth century the Yamani tribes followed the lead of the Hina tribe and the Nizar tribes followed the Bani Ghafir. Over the centuries, the confederations have assumed religious attributes as well with the Ghafiri often described as Sunni and the Hinawi as Ibadi.

Like tribalism, the alliance system is not static, and these characterizations will not hold for every tribe. Tribes change confederations, with the most often cited being the Ghafiri who later became Hinawi. Also, the two major Ghafiri tribes, the Bani Riyam and the Ibriyin, are strongly Ibadi rather than Sunni. The alliance system has performed a very important function in Omani history for while every tribal dispute does have the potential to become a national conflict, as with the two civil wars, the threat of such an occurrence has helped to keep a lid on disputes. Furthermore, the Hinawi and Ghafiri can and have cooperated to unify the country behind a strong central government.

### Other Ethnic Groups

Although Arabs dominate the Oman region and their social organization and religion set the standard for the entire country, other ethnic groups have flourished in the sultanate. The Ru'us al-Jibal region is inhabited entirely by a little-known people called the Shihuh, a composite group of mysterious origins that has been equated with the Shuhites of the Old Testament. The largest component of the Shihuh, divided between the Bani Hadiya and Bani Shatair tribes, claims descent from the original Arab settlers or Oman but speaks an Arabic dialect unintelligible to other Arabs. A second component is the Dhahriyin, who also claim to be Arab and deny that they are Shihuh but are dominated by the tribe. Finally, the Kumazarah, most prominent on the east side of Ru'us al-Jibal and allied with the Shatair, speak a Persian dialect and may be of Baluchi origin. In religion the Shihuh are Sunni, but they also include some animistic practices in their observances.

About 30,000 Baluchis, principally from the Huti and Zidgali (Jidgali) tribes, have settled in Oman from the Makran Coast of Pakistan. Most Baluchis were brought to Oman as mercenaries and remained an important part of the military until very recently. Other members of the community have served as day laborers, especially in the port towns. Accordingly, the community has been concentrated in the Capital Area with some Baluchis found along the Batinah, and a small group, the Bani Balush, settled in Sirr where they represent the remnants of a failed eighteenth-century military campaign and have been assimilated into the Arab tribal system. The community is Sunni and has had little success in integrating into Omani society.

Several immigrant Indian communities have settled in Oman, primarily in Muscat, Matrah, and the towns of the Batinah. Until 1970 Omani commerce was dominated by Hindu Banians, most of whom were from the Bhattia caste from Kutch. Hindus have been residing in Oman since at least the sixteenth century, and during the nineteenth century several thousand settled in Muscat and Matrah where they served as importers and exporters, agents for local merchants, government contractors, and bankers. Socially, they have retained their distinctive dress and customs. The community was granted religious freedom in Muscat, where it built several temples and other religious buildings and maintained a herd of cattle to meet its dietary needs. Since 1970 the resident community has shrunk because citizenship was denied to all but a select few and because new business laws that favor Omani nationals have hurt Hindu commercial activities.

A second group of resident Indians is the Liwatiyah. The group has obscure origins possibly in Sind, India, although some members may be remnants of Persian gypsies. During the nineteenth century, the Liwatiyah Indians were Khojahs (Ismaili Shi'as), but the community broke with the Agha Khan during the 1860s and the majority converted to Ithna-'ashari Shi'ism. The community, although very active in commerce in Matrah, was historically extremely exclusive, residing in a walled ghetto in Matrah known as Sur Liwatiyah to which all outsiders were denied access. The community also had its own court system and schools. Since 1970, the Liwatiyah have made active efforts to become assimilated into Omani society: Most have left the Sur and adopted Arabic language and dress.

Several smaller minority groups can also be found in Oman. The Bayasira, a widely spread group, may represent the original inhabitants of Oman. Although organized into tribes, the members have never been accepted by the Arab tribal structure and remain second-class clients. A similar group is the Zatutis, who are considered non-Arabs but of unknown origin; according to one opinion, they are northern Arabian gypsies whereas another suggests that they have Indian origins. Zatutis are active in carpentry and metal work trades in the larger towns. A small Shi'ite community known as Baharnah lives in Muscat and Matrah. Active in commerce, the Baharnah came to Oman in the nineteenth century from Persia and claim to be the original inhabitants of Bahrain, from which they were expelled following the Arab conquest of that island in 1783. Finally, the Sonora are Sunni Muslims of the Bohra caste from India who live in the Capital Area and engage primarily in gold and silver working.

Most of Dhofar's people are Arab, although Sunni rather than Ibadi. Along the coast several migrant groups, primarily from the Hadramaut region of Yemen, have become established. The Al-Kathir, with their three large clans, the Shanfari, Rawwas, and Marhun, clearly dominate, but there are also groups of Hadrami Sayyids, descendants of the Prophet Muhammad known locally as Hashmiyin, and Yafa'i tribespeople. Other groups include descendants of African slaves and remnants of the Moplahs, Indian Muslims of Hadrami descent who ruled Dhofar briefly in the nineteenth century.

The most significant group in Dhofar, however, is the Jibalis. Considered Arabs, the Jibalis speak dialects of Arabic very closely akin to ancient south Arabic, which are unintelligible to their Omani compatriots. This group is divided among the Qara, who also live on the Salalah Plain, and their clients the Shahara, who may be the original inhabitants of Dhofar, and a small group of Mahra concentrated in the Jabal Samhan. A related group is the Harasis who roam the Jiddat al-Harasis region and speak a dialect of Mahra called Harsusi.

## TRADITIONAL ECONOMY

Agriculture has long been the basis of Omani society. Farmers were able to overcome poor soil and a shortage of water to grow dates, limes, and other fruits and vegetables. Fishing supplemented agriculture along the coast, and 5 percent of the population followed a nomadic life-style. Some traditional manufacturing has also been conducted, with pottery, weaving, metal work, ship building, and several other handicrafts being important activities.

Although less than 1 percent of the sultanate's land is cultivatable, agriculture is by far the most important economic activity in the country, accounting for the livelihood of 85 percent of the people. The Omani farmer is beset with two major obstacles. The first is a lack of good soil. Agriculture is limited to outwash plains, known as *sails*, located at the mouths of wadis where silt eroded from the mountains by runoff has been deposited. These sails might be quite small, as in Ru'us al-Jibal or some parts of interior Oman, or extend over relatively large areas, such as the Batinah and Salalah plains or the Jawf in Oman. Even the soils in these areas are of very poor quality, with high calcium content, low moisture retention, low organic content, and high deterioration rates.

A second problem is the lack of water. The sultanate lies on the boundary of the Saharo-Arabico subtropical system and the Indian Ocean monsoon. This location has meant that the country receives slightly more rainfall than the rest of Arabia but that that rainfall is seasonal (July and December), irregular (droughts are common), and localized. With little vegetation or soil, runoff tends to be rapid, and evaporation rates are much higher than participation levels so that even where rain is absorbed, dry-land farming is impossible. Irrigation is an absolute necessity.

Fortunately, some of the rainfall finds its way into aquifers in the mountains or is retained in the gravels of the wadis and from there enters the water table so that water is available in wells. Along the Batinah and the Salalah Plain, where the water table is near the surface and ground water is relatively plentiful, traditional tube wells serve irrigation needs. However, in Ru'us al Jibal and in places in which water resources are not readily available or plentiful, Shihuh farmers, especially those in the mountains, have depended on collecting runoff in cisterns and storing the water for irrigation.

### Irrigation Systems

In interior Oman much more elaborate irrigation systems known as *aflaj* (s. *falaj*) have been devised. Aflaj use channels to bring water from a distance to the farmers' fields. One source is the water that flows within the gravels below the surface of the wadi bed, which is collected in tanks and carried to the village by a channel. Another source is ground water, usually from an underground spring. This type of falaj is much more difficult to construct as it first requires locating the water source, sinking a well or wells, and then digging a *qanat* (tunnel) to bring the water to the surface channel that carries the water to the village.

Falaj construction is attributed to Persian settlers of ancient times, but the maintenance of old aflaj and the need for new have required that Arabs learn these skills. The Awamir tribe, from around Manah in Jawf, have become falaj specialists, both in divining water and in digging *qanats*, usually with hammer and chisel. Their work has left a distinctive mark on the Omani landscape: Most villages are surrounded by lines of what appear to be pot holes, which are actually the access shafts that provide ventilation and facilitate the removal of excavated materials during initial construction and later repair of the qanats.

Aflaj are strictly regulated to ensure proper and equitable use of the precious water. Surface channels are generally covered to reduce evaporation losses, prevent pollution, and control access. The last is especially important: The water is first used for drinking, then for bathing, and then for irrigation. Falaj water is not diverted to private dwellings (which must depend on wells); once the water enters the village it is used to irrigate crops. Water rights are purchased with the operation of the system and include the recording of rights and distribution of water overseen by a village official.

### Crops

With the water provided by the aflaj and wells Omani farmers have planted a variety of produce, much of which was introduced from India. In interior Oman wheat, alfalfa, and sugar are grown; the Batinah produces limes, bananas, mangoes; Jabal al-Akhdar is famous for its grapes, pomegranates, and apricots; in Dhofar the main crops are coconuts, sorghum, and sweet potatoes; and farmers in Ja'lan even grow a little rice. However, by far the most important single crop is the date, accounting for nearly 70 percent of Omani agricultural production. The hot, dry Omani climate with irrigated agriculture is ideally suited to the date palm, which according to an Arab proverb needs to have its feet in the water and head in the fire, and the country boasts innumerable varieties that connoisseurs in Oman rate much like French gourmands do their wines.

The importance of the date palm and dates to Oman cannot be overstated. Dates were the staff of life until recent times, accounting for an estimated half of the people's caloric intake. The considerable surplus was Oman's main export commodity, with the bulk going to India. Date production provided seasonable employment as the dates had to be prepared and packed for shipment. By-products also served a myriad of purposes: building materials, matting, animal fodder, and even shade for the protection of other fruit and vegetable plants.

Agriculture, like the aflaj, resulted in the creation of a specialized caste, the Bidar. Although these people, like the Bayasir, may represent the remnants of the pre-Arab population, they have been assimilated into the tribal structure so that in modern times the designation Bidar has become purely occupational. The Bidar are not just farmers, however; they are technically specialists in irrigating and tending date palms, including fertilizing, trimming, pollinating, and harvesting. Menial farming chores are left to others.

### Supplements to Farming

Along the Batinah farming has historically been supplemented by fishing. The Omani coast lies within a zone of upswelling, mineral rich cold water that, when it interacts with the hot Arabian sun, results in one of the richest fishing grounds in the world. The great variety of fish, including sardines, shark, and tuna, has been an important part of the economy: Fish, consumed both fresh and dried, are an important source of protein and fish and fish by-products are used for fertilizer and cattle feed. The surplus is traded both domestically with the interior people for dates and other produce and internationally, with shark fin going to China and fish meal to Sri Lanka, India, and even Europe.

Most farmers maintain small numbers of animals: goats and sheep for milk, meat, wool, and hides, a donkey for transport, and maybe a cow or, rarely, a horse. About 5 percent of the people follow some form of nomadism. Several traditional bedouin groups exist—most notably the Wahiba, Duru', Janaba, Awamir, Bait Kathir, and Harasis—whose economies are based on tending goats and camels and who roam within roughly defined tribal territories in the desert. Most bedouins in Oman spend their summers camped near villages where they own date gardens tended by Bidars.

Distinctive nomadic groups include the Shawawi of northern Oman and the Jibalis of Dhofar. The Shawawi are mostly goat herders who inhabit temporary camps among which they rotate regularly. Their migrations are normally over very small distances and appear to be more a matter of superstition or personal convenience than for the benefit of their herds. The Jibalis are unique in that they tend distinctive small cattle. Their migrations generally take them to the northern slopes where they inhabit caves during the wet season from June to October and then back to the southern slopes during the dry months of winter. The Shihuh are also seasonable nomads moving from the mountains to the coast during the summer dry season in Ru'us al-Jibal.

## CRAFTS, ARTS, AND LITERATURE

Although Oman lacks such raw materials as cotton, lumber, and metals, which have to be imported, and its products must compete against manufactured imports from India, Europe, and the United States, a few Omanis have made their living as craftspeople and artisans. Islamic strictures against representation of living forms have limited artistic activities, but the religion has inspired literary composition, especially legal works and history. More popular literature includes poetry and folktales.

Omani architecture draws on both Middle Eastern and Indian traditions. The most widely known buildings, depicted on Omani postage stamps, are the forts that dominate major towns such as Muscat, Matrah, Sohar, Hazm, Rustaq, and Nizwa. Domestic architecture has not been completely ignored. The palaces at Jabrin and Birka demonstrate the peak of Omani design; the better preserved structure at Jabrin contains outstanding examples of decorative art and craft such as fine wood carvings, painted decorations, and carved plaster work using calligraphy and geometric and vegetation designs. All show Persian and Indian influence, raising speculation that the work was done by foreign artisans.

Dwellings of the common people are much simpler in design; they have few rooms, usually including a public room, women's quarters, and open-air kitchen and storage room built around an open courtyard. Even these dwellings have carved woodwork and painted decorations. Also of note are the palm frond houses (*barastis*) found on the Batina coast. These woven houses are inexpensive and ideally suited to the coastal climate as they enable the inhabitants to take advantage of onshore breezes. Carpentry is done mostly by Zatutis who also build plows and other equipment for farmers and mushroom-shaped storage containers.

Shipbuilding, a trade little practiced today, was done in Sur and Matrah. Many kinds of ships, known generically as dhows, were built, from large sea-going vessels based on European designs to the double-ended boats used for fishing along the entire Omani coast. Omani shipbuilders traditionally worked without plans and were adept at sewing rather than nailing their craft together. Craftspeople along the Batina also built small surf fishing boats from palm fronds sewn together.

Metalworking, both in copper and silver, was widely practiced throughout Oman. Nizwa served as the center of this industry, and Bahla and Matrah were secondary areas. Tinned copper containers, including bowls, plates, coffee pots, and various utensils, generally are decorated with simple geometric designs or more elaborate vegetation patterns, again showing Indian and Persian influences. Silverworking products include jewelry, *khanjars* (the curved daggers worn by every Omani adult male), and small storage containers and the decoration of imported rifles and swords.

Pottery for local use was traditionally made in nearly every Omani town. Bahla served as the main production center for large vessels and some specialty items, and its wares were found throughout Oman even in medieval times. Omani pottery is usually simple and unglazed with little decoration. The exceptions to this are the incense burners manufactured in Dhofar in various shapes and sizes with elaborate designs.

Although most clothing was fashioned from cotton sheeting imported from India and the United States, Oman did develop an indigenous weaving and dying industry. Locally grown and imported cotton was spun for weaving into loin cloths worn beneath a cotton robe, whereas Bedouins provided goat-hair thread for woven carpets, saddlebags, and cloaks. Nearly every town supported weavers, and certain towns produced specialty items, such as Bahla's goat-hair cloaks, Samail's cotton cloth, and Matrah's stiped cloth. Firq, near Nizwa, was famous for its indigo dying, using imported raw materials, and the large dye pots used for dying can still be seen. Embroidery was the one craft traditionally practiced by women, who utilized their skills in decorating the skull caps worn by small boys and some men.

Ibadism, like Islam in general, dictates against most arts and music so that most creative endeavors have been directed toward literary activities, especially law and history. As the world's leading center of Ibadism, Oman's religious scholars have been responsible for several major compendia of case law, including the *Qamus al-Sharia*, the *Bayan al-Sharia*, and the *Musannaf*. Historical works of note include the anonymous *Kashf al-Juma'*, Abdullah b. Humaid al-Salimi's *Tuhfat al-Ayan*, which covers Omani history to the early twentieth century, and his son Muhammad al-Salimi's *Nahda al-Ayan*, which continues the work to the 1950s.

Besides these national epics, Oman also has quite a lively tradition of popular literature. Several poets have national reputations and each town has its local legends and folktales. The popular stories usually focus on the deeds of witches and spirits, but some contain legends of giants or even accounts out of local history. Some cities are known for their particular literary specialties; for instance, Bahla is the center of black magic in Oman.

Efforts have been made since the mid-1970s to preserve Oman's cultural and artistic heritage. The ministry of national heritage and culture has been active in collecting and publishing important scholarly works and has set up a national library and archive to preserve manuscript materials. Also, the ministry has assumed control over most historic monuments, such as Jabrin and many of the forts, and is supervising restoration of those buildings. In addition, local craftspeople, especially weavers and potterers, have been encouraged to preserve traditional crafts.

# 2

# Ancient and Medieval History

Recent archaeological work conducted in Oman has traced the existence of settled agriculture in the country to the late fourth century B.C. and confirmed the long-held theory that Oman was ancient Magan (Makkan), the principal supplier of copper to Sumer. Later, during the Achaemenid Empire, Oman was colonized by Persians who brought with them their irrigation system and began the maritime development of the Batinah coast. The coming of Islam resulted in the expulsion of the Persians as Arab immigrants gained control of Oman. For a brief period in the ninth century A.D., however, the country generally fell within the orbit of larger and more powerful neighbors such as the Umayyads, the Abbasids, and a succession of Persian overlords. The interior, where a distinctive national consciousness based on Ibadism and an elected imamate had developed, remained more or less independent, whereas coastal cities such as Sohar and Qalhat rose to international prominence as commercial centers. Then in the sixteenth century the Portuguese asserted their control over coastal Oman. Finally, in 1640 a new era in Omani history commenced with the election of an imam who sought to unify the entire country.

## MAGAN AND MAZUN

Settled agriculture first appeared in Oman in the late fourth–early third millennium B.C. Although there is evidence, in the form of cultural influences and trade objects, of contact between Oman and Mesopotamia in the early phase (3200–2600 B.C.), confusingly referred to as Jamdat Nasr after a contemporary Iraqi culture, the Omani culture is distinct and certainly does not represent a Mesopotamian colony. Its latter phase (2600–1800 B.C.), known as Umm al-Nar after an archaeological site near Abu Dhabi where the culture was first discovered, centered on interior Oman and maintained cultural and commercial links with both Sumer and southeastern Iran with Umm al-Nar representing a maritime outpost.

Access shafts to a qanat. Qanats (underground water channels) were introduced to Oman by Persian colonists in the seventh century B.C. as part of the falaj irrigation system. These qanats enable Omani farmers to tap into distant groundwater sources and bring that water to their gardens.

### Umm al-Nar

Archaeological surveys and preliminary excavations in Oman point to the Jawf region in the western Hajar Mountains as the core area of ancient Omani civilization in which major settlements ran from Julfar on the Gulf coast in the north along the western side of the mountains to Sharqiyah in the south. All the settlement sites are located on the banks of wadis so that farmers could rely on natural runoff after precipitation or possibly use artificial irrigation by trapping water and silt behind humanmade barrages. There is also speculation that the Omani climate was wetter during the third millennium B.C. because the monsoon might have been slightly more northerly.

The cultures of these settlers were fairly advanced. Farmers were planting wheat, barley, and sorghum, the last introduced from Africa, and there is evidence of date cultivation. The camel had been domesticated. Houses seem to have been made of stone, and at least three specialized buildings existed: the distinctive Umm al-Nar graves for mass burials; central, elevated, walled structures that served either ceremonial or defensive purposes; and towers, very similar to those that dot the modern Omani landscape, associated with either water distribution or defense. A principal activity of all third-millennium settlements was copper smelting. Some of this copper was used locally, but much was traded to Mesopotamia, and Oman was part of a widespread trading network that included Sumer, the Indus valley (ancient Meluhha), and Africa.

Outside of the Jawf, Sharqiyah, and the western Hajar, the spread of civilization lagged behind. Stone-age settlements, again always situated on the banks of wadis or near modern-day wells but in areas that are today uninhabited, and flint mine and factory areas are spread throughout Oman from Dhofar to the north. Most are impossible to date. The Batinah coast also shows little evidence of development with only one site near Sohar, which significantly shows no evidence of maritime activity, and protohistoric fishing communities on the coast near Muscat and Quriyat.

### Persian Expansion

By the end of the third millennium, camel nomadism began to replace settled agriculture as a way of life in Oman, probably as a result of desiccation of the climate. The copper trade ended and urbanized life disappeared. Nearly a thousand years passed before farming settlements again appeared in Oman. This second phase in civilization in Oman is associated with Persian expansion into the Arabian Peninsula and the development of Oman's irrigation system based on the falaj. The first efforts to develop an irrigation system in Oman are traced to the eighth or seventh century B.C. when a cut and cover technique was used in the area of ancient Magan. The first true qanats date to the Achaemenid occupation of Oman with these Persians developing the old cultivated area from Julfar to the Sharqiyah. After the destruction of the Achaemenids by Alexander the Great, Oman reverted to an independent existence though still closely tied to southeast Persia.

By the first century A.D. demographics of Oman began to change significantly as Arab migrants from western Arabia began to arrive. A first wave of Arabs began settling in the Ja'lan region on the fringes of the Rub al-Khali and Wahiba deserts, the settled agricultural area of the Jawf, and eventually all the desert borderlands on the western side of the mountains. These Arabs, nominally under the leadership of the Bani Hina tribe, were little involved with the existing settlers. A second wave, coming from the north and under the control of the Bani Ma'awal, increased pressure on the limited resources available to the Arabs, forcing them into the settled mountain zone regions of Tu'am, Sirr, and the Jabal al-Akhdar and even into the eastern slopes of the mountains in Ghadaf.

Wadi Mistal in the Ghadaf. Wadis (dry river beds) such as Wadi Mistal crisscross the mountainous terrain of Oman and help to facilitate communication throughout the country.

These Arab migrations coincided with an increasing Persian penetration of Oman by the Sassanids under Ardashir I (226–241). Unlike the Achaemenids, the Sassanids were interested primarily in the Batinah and maritime trade. The focal point of ther Arabian province of Mazun was Omana (Sohar) where the governor resided as did the main garrison; it was even the seat of a Nestorian bishopric. Omana was the principal port in the Persian maritime province of Ard al-Hind as well as one of the traditional market centers of pre-Islamic Arabia. The Sassanids also developed the Batinah, where their second main town was Dama near modern Sib, and the Ghadaf. Rustaq served as the administrative and garrison town in this new area of extensive land and falaj development; the site was chosen because of its easy access to both Omana and Dama and its location near the heart of Ma'awal territory to the east. Although the Sassanid empire still included the interior, where it introduced the cemented falaj, it exercised little authority there.

In the sixth century the Sassanid Shah Kawadh (488–531) attempted to check Arab encroachments on Persian lands but with little success. Arab legend describes a great battle fought between Arabs and Persians at Salut near Bahla, in which the Persians were defeated and agreed to withdraw from Oman all except 4,000 settlers. Before leaving, the Persians reportedly destroyed many aflaj. There are elements of truth in the Arab legend. Arab raids on Persian settlements did no doubt result in some victories, although the Persians were never driven from the interior. The Arabs did receive recognition of a quasi-independence during the administrative reforms of Anushirvan (531–579) when the shaikh of the Ma'awal was recognized as *julanda* over the Arabs. The julanda (Arabian leader) reported to a Sassanid provincial governor at Rustaq. In interior Oman the Persians continued to occupy the major towns whereas the Arabs inhabited the countryside and had their main settlements at Buraimi, considered to be the Arab capital, and on the coast at Dibba, the main market center. The so-called falaj destruction was attributed more to poor maintenance by the Arabs than to any intentional devastation by the Persians.

Dhofar's prehistory and ancient history are not nearly as well documented as those of northern Oman. Even in ancient times, though, the region was famous for its frankincense, which was highly valued in the markets of the Mediterranean. To gain control of that trade, in the first century B.C. King Il'ad Yalut I of Shabwa in the Hadramaut sent an expedition to the Dhofari coast to construct a fortress, harbor, and town. The immigrants built the city of SMHRM (translated variously as Samaramm, Sumhuram) in Khor Rori near modern Taqa. The town, known to the Greeks as Moscha, continued to flourish until the third century, when Dhofar again disappeared from the pages of history.

### THE EARLY ISLAMIC PERIOD

Islam brought tremendous change to Oman. In 630 the Prophet Muhammad's envoy, Amr ibn al-'As, met with the Julandas Abd and Jaifar and gained their submission to the new faith. This was followed by the general concurrence of the Arab shaikhs and the sending of a delegation to Medina. Amr b. al-'As remained in Oman, instructing the Arabs in their new religion and encouraging them to take action against the Persians. Accordingly, and not reluctantly, the Persians were invited to submit to Allah or face destruction. When they refused, Rustaq was attacked and captured, and the Persian governor was killed. The victorious Arabs then advanced on Sohar where the Persian governor decided not to resist, and with the promise of safe conduct, the Sassanids withdrew to Iran. Oman became Muslim and Arab.

Muhammad's policy in Oman was to apply the hand of Muslim government very lightly, most notably with regard to taxation; *zakat* (taxes) collected in Oman remained there for distribution to the poor with no remittances to Medina. Abu Bakr changed the policy when he

became caliph, and this proved to be the motive for a revolt against
Medina that threatened to erupt into a general tribal uprising against
Islam. One Dhu al-Taj (a Persian title) Lakit b. Malik led the opposition
while the julandas held firm with Medina. Abu Bakr sent Ikrima b. Abi
Jahl, Hudaifa b. Muhsin, and Afraja b. Harthima to reinforce the Omani
Muslims. After gaining the surrender of some of Lakit's tribal allies in
the Sohar area, the rebel stronghold at Dibba was attacked and destroyed.
Ikrima marched on to the Hadramaut, and Arfaja returned to Medina
with a fifth of the booty won in the victory, which was due to the
government. Hudaifa remained in Oman as governor.

Throughout the remainder of the Rashidun caliphate, Oman remained a peaceful backwater within the ever growing Muslim empire.
Control of the province remained in the hands of the julanda, officially
under the governor of Bahrain (eastern Arabia). Omanis played a
prominent role in the conquest of Persia and in preliminary raids on
western India, and an occasional Omani, such as Muhallab b. Abi Sufra,
distinguished himself in military action.

An indication of things to come occurred in 684 when during an
uprising the Kharijites temporarily took control of Oman. Although the
Julandas Sa'id and Sulaiman b. Abbad b. Abd were able to suppress
the revolt, Oman, lacking any control from Damascus, increasingly
became a zone of refuge for dissident groups, especially Kharijites, and
an area of constantly quarreling tribes. When this situation came to the
notice of the Umayyad governor of Iraq, al-Hajjaj b. Yusuf, he resolved
to do something about it. In about 697 an expedition was sent to Oman,
but it was defeated by the Omanis in Wadi Hatat. A second expedition
was sent by land and sea. Sulaiman b. Abbad was able to defeat the
land forces near Abu Dhabi, but the main column landed near Birka.
There Sa'id b. Abbad was defeated, and he retreated to the Jabal al-
Akhdar. Sulaiman marched to the Batinah and pursued the Umayyad
army up Wadi Sama'il, where he too was defeated. When more reinforcements arrived at Julfar, the julandas realized their desperate situation
and fled to East Africa.

Al-Hajjaj's conquest of Oman did little to mitigate the problems
that had caused the military campaign in the first place: The governor
of Iraq used Oman as an area of exile and sent a number of prominent
Ibadis there. After al-Hajjaj's death, when the Muhallabis gained control
of Iraqi affairs, Oman was again virtually ignored by the central
administration and the julandas reassumed control of political affairs.
The situation soon reverted to the chaos that had drawn al-Hajjaj's
attention in the first place. Ibadi propaganda, tribal squabbling, the
collapse of caliphal authority, and a new matter—divisions within the
julanda clan—all contributed to the problem.

## THE IBADI IMAMATE

The establishment of the Abbasid Caliphate and its appointment of a governor did not help the situation. The Baghdad government sent Bani Hina Ibadi sympathizers to Oman, whose tacit support led the Ibadi clerics in Oman to seek to achieve their ideal of an elected imamate. Drawing on divisions within the julanda ruling family but recognizing the general respect afforded that clan, Julanda b. Masud was accordingly proclaimed imam in 750. The new imam immediately faced two problems: the opposition of the Omani tribes, including his own, which had become used to independence, and an Abbasid invasion. The imam was able to overcome the first problem by killing his rivals in the Julanda clan; the external threat provided by the Abbasid invasion served to unite the tribes behind him.

### The Abbasids

Dealing with the Abbasids proved to be far more difficult. The Abbasid attack on Oman had nothing to do with either Oman or the election of the imam. In 751 the caliph al-Saffah dispatched an army to Persia to eliminate the Sufriya Kharijites, who like the Ibadis were a moderate branch of that sect. They had fled to Julfar where they were defeated by the Omanis and their leader was killed. The Abbasid army continued its pursuit of the Kharijites to Oman and, after learning of the destruction of the Sufriya, demanded the submission of the Omanis. Julanda b. Masud refused, the Abbasids attacked, and the Omanis were defeated and Julanda killed. The first imamate came to an end.

Following the collapse of the first imamate, the Abbasids were content to leave Omani affairs in the hands of the julanda. The Omani tribes had other ideas. Rashid b. al-Nazr, grandson of Sa'id b. Abbad, became the julanda but had to suppress a tribal revolt in the Ghadaf. Then in 762 Rashid barely survived a tribal attack on Nizwa. Finally in 794 Ibadi opposition solidified with the election of Muhammad b. Abdallah b. Abi Affan as imam. Although Ibn Abi Affan was a controversial choice, he did succeed in defeating the julandas in the Dhahirah, their center of support, thereby ending julanda rule in Oman. Soon after the victory Muhammad b. Abdallah was deposed, and in 795 al-Warith b. Ka'b al-Kharusi was elected imam in his place.

### Omani Victory and Civil War

Warith's imamate (795–806) marks the beginning of a golden age of the medieval imamate in Oman. The new imam's first duty was to overcome an invasion sent by Harun al-Rashid, which landed near Sohar. The Omanis were victorious. Al-Rashid planned a second invasion, but when the imam began sending an annual tribute, the caliph's anger was assuaged and Oman lived in peace. Warith died in a flood in Nizwa, and the ulema took three years to choose his successor. The new imam, Ghassan b. Abdallah al-Yahmadi, was an outstanding choice: He is remembered for developing an Omani navy to protect merchants from pirates on the Indian coast and for improving the falaj system. When he died in 823 he was succeeded by Abd al-Malik b. Hamid (823–842), Muhanna b. Jaifar al-Yahmadi (842–851), and Salt b. Malik al-Yahmadi (851–886), who were known as just rulers who presided over a long period of economic development and domestic stability— save for a last ditch attempt by the julanda to reassert their authority during the imamate of Muhanna.

This golden age came suddenly to a close when in 886 Salt b. Malik was driven from Nizwa in a revolt led by one Musa b. Musa, which introduced seven years of civil war. Musa, with the support of the Yemeni Ibadi tribes, became the power behind the imamate and instituted intolerant policies toward Oman's Sunni tribes (primarily northern ones) and their Nizari allies. Even after Musa died in 890 the suppression of the Sunnis continued. The hard-pressed Nizaris, having been defeated at Rustaq and Tanuf, ultimately turned to the Abbasid governor of Bahrain, Muhammad b. Nur, for relief. Muhammad received caliphal permission to invade Oman and arrived in Buraimi in 893 to find the imamate completely discredited and the country in chaos. A second army arrived by sea at Julfar, and the Abbasids marched on Nizwa. The imam, Azzan b. Tamim, had withdrawn from his capital to prepare a defense at Samad in Sharqiyah. Muhammad b. Nur made short work of his force, and the imam's head was sent to the caliph as a present while Oman was ruthlessly pacified.

Muhammad b. Nur's excesses not only gained him the name bin Bur (wasteland) in the Omani chronicles; they also unified Omani opposition. Resistance was organized by Ahif b. Hamham al-Hina'i, who succeeded in driving Muhammad from Nizwa and pursuing him to the Batinah. Except for the timely arrival of reinforcements, Muhammad would have been defeated; instead the Omanis suffered a devastating loss in which Ahif was killed. Muhammad b. Nur returned to Nizwa and took his revenge on the Ibadi community by destroying property, killing followers, and burning books. Muhammad left Oman in 896, leaving behind Ahmad b. Hilal as governor in Nizwa. Ahmad was ultimately driven from the interior and forced to reside in Sohar.

A more long-lasting impact of the Omani civil war was a split within the ulema over the issue of deposing the imam. Two factions arose, one centered in Nizwa, which recognized the propriety of deposing an imam, and the other in Rustaq, which rejected that theory. The result was that no agreement could be reached on an imam. A series of imams, probably representing the successive rise and fall of military leaders, was elected and deposed during a long dark age for interior Oman in which it was subjected to waves of foreign invasions from the Saffarids, Qarmatians, Abbasids, and Buyids, and the focus of Omani history shifted to the Batinah coast.

## SOHAR AND QALHAT

While the tribes and imams quarreled over the interior, coastal Oman began to flourish under foreign rule and Sohar became the principal entrepôt for the western Indian Ocean trade. Sohar had first risen to prominence under the Persians in pre-Islamic times and had continued to be an important trade center up to the tenth century; an eighth-century Omani from Sohar named Abu Ubayda Abdallah al-Qasim was the first documented Arab traveler to China.

### Rise of Sohar

Sohar's importance in the tenth century had a series of causes. First, the disruptions in the Gulf brought about by the Abbasid civil war and the constant power struggle in southern Iraq and Iran meant that few ships would venture there unescorted. Sohar came to serve as the gathering point for convoys to Iraq in much the same way as Muscat had in the eighteenth and nineteenth centuries. Furthermore, although Sohar was certainly not rich in resources nor did it have a large market, it did possess some exports such as copper (with the redevelopment of the ancient mines at Lasail), horses, and dried fruit and dates and was a good provisioning point because it was the best watered and most fertile point on the coast. Finally, the absence of a suitable harbor was outweighed by an advantageous location vis-à-vis the wind systems of both the Gulf and the Indian Ocean monsoon. Sohar, unlike better anchorages on the Persian coast, was the best place to catch the winds for either India or Africa.

Sohar's rise to glory is associated with the rule of Ahmad b. Hilal, Muhammad b. Nur's former deputy in Nizwa, who ruled the port until 918, and the Wajihids, who assumed control of the port following its conquest by their Qarmatian allies in 929. Ahmad b. Hilal's reputation for supporting trade is evidenced by his supposed intervention in preventing an attempt by the caliph to confiscate the property of a wealthy Jewish merchant in Sohar—action that he thought would cause merchants to leave Sohar—and by the gifts, including a talking mynah bird, that were sent to Baghdad. During Wajihid rule (929–965) the Sohari navy was a dominant force in the Gulf region, with Yusuf b.

Wajih providing naval support for a Qarmatian attack on Basra in 942 and his son Muhammad doing likewise in 953. Other Gulf ports, most notably Siraf, were forced to defend themselves against the Wajihids. Outside the Gulf region, the Omani fleet's main focus was East Africa and Madagascar where it traded for slaves, gold, ivory, shell, and hides; India appears to have been a secondary trading partner.

### Omani Domestic Upheaval

Sohar's brief era of glory ended soon after 953 when the Wajihids were overthrown in a palace coup by one of their slaves named Nafi. Although a Qarmatian invasion in 963 ended Nafi's ten-year reign, Qarmatian attempts to subdue interior Oman, including the murders of eighty Ibadi qadis, so alienated the Omanis that the Bahrainis were soon driven out. That allowed Muiz al-Dawla Buwayhi to assert Buyid control over Oman in 965. The Buyid army, commanded by Adud al-Dawla, destroyed both Sohar and the Omani fleet. Then in 971 when Adud al-Dawla was suppressing a revolt of the Buyid garrison in Sohar, the port was again destroyed. Buyid actions were motivated almost exclusively by the desire to eliminate any competition for their port of Siraf, which soon replaced Sohar as the Gulf entrepôt.

Interior Oman continued to experience difficulties with domestic upheaval and repeated foreign invasions. An attempt to expel the Buyids in 972 succeeded only in securing Persian control over the interior, and when Samsam al-Dawla attempted to use Oman as a base for the overthrow of Adud al-Dawla in 984 the country again suffered. There was a brief resurgence when the ulema was able to agree on the election of al-Khalil b. Shadhan (c. 1016–1029), and his successor Rashid b. Sa'id (1029–1053) was finally able to expel the Buyids. The Ibadi ulema soon reverted to its quarreling and began electing a new series of rival imams whose names, dates, and even order are a mystery to the Omani chroniclers. Eventually the imamate disappeared, and the interior came to be controlled by tyrants (jabara) from the Nabahana tribe. The coast continued under Persian rule, followed by periods of Seljuk and Ghuz rule from Kirman, although in both cases control seems to have been limited to the coast.

### Rise of Qalhat

While Oman was experiencing these difficulties, Dhofar again began to assume some importance. During early medieval times Dhofar's main port seems to have been located near the present town of Mirbat. Then in the late tenth century the Persian Minjui dynasty assumed control of the region and built a new capital at al-Balid, within present-day Salalah. In 1207 the Manjui were overthrown by Ahmad b. Abdallah

Hilltop tower. Built on nearly every strategic hilltop in Oman, stone towers were used historically to defend villages and mountain passes. The design of these towers has been traced to the earliest cultures in Oman.

al-Habudi, a rich merchant and shipowner-cum-*wazir* (prime minister) for the Minjui. Al-Habudi destroyed al-Balid and built an entire new city called Zafar in 1221. Under the Habudi dynasty Zafar reached its peak as a result of the shifting of trade routes to the east and its being a source of horses and frankincense for markets as far afield as China and Europe. Despite an attempt by Mahmud b. Ahmad al-Qusi, the ruler of Qalhat, to conquer the town in 1261, the Habudis ruled until 1278 when they were replaced by the Yemeni Rasulids, who ruled for 150 years and under whom Zafar continued to flourish. With the fall of the Rasulids, Zafar came to be controlled by a Kathiri dynasty that ruled from Shihr in Hadramaut. The Kathiri rulers banned all trade in horses and frankincense from Zafar—a move designed to encourage the growth of their own capital—which ended Zafar commercial importance.

In the early thirteenth century Qalhat developed into the entrepôt for the Gulf trade. The collapse of Buyid power had again thrown the Gulf region into chaos and allowed minor dynasties throughout the region to flourish and extend their own commercial networks. Also, more and more trade was being directed to Egypt. Qalhat's southerly location on the Oman coast made it ideally suited to serve this new trade, and the port flourished, first under the Khwarizmis, who took control of the Omani coast about 1215, and then under a native Omani, Mahmud b. Ahmad al-Qusi. Mahmud, taking advantage of the Mongol invasions of Persia, established his authority from Hormuz to Dhofar and developed Qalhat as the main entrepôt, although it certainly never reached the level of tenth-century Sohar.

Mahmud had grander plans. His attempt to conquer Oman in 1262 failed as his army was swallowed up in the desert, but a raid on the town of Zafar in Dhofar succeeded in plundering that town, although Mahmud was not able to hold it. Qalhat remained an important entrepôt until the mid-fourteenth century, by which time it was being replaced by Muscat. Qalhat also faced stiff competition from Hormuz. An earth-quake that devastated the city in the fourteenth century and its occupation and eventual destruction by the Portuguese a century and a half later spelled the end for Qalhat, which to this day is virtually deserted.

### THE PORTUGUESE

The final era in Oman's medieval history is marked by the arrival of the first European threat to the country, the Portuguese. Afonso de Alboquerque arrived off the Omani coast in August 1507 and explored from Ras al-Hadd to Sur and destroyed any native craft that he found. The Portuguese fleet finally anchored off Qalhat, which offered no resistance and promised submission to Portuguese authority once de

Traditional large house. Fortified houses, common throughout interior Oman, allow tribal leaders and large landowners to house entire extended families within their stone walls and still have sufficient room for storage, servants' quarters, and guest accommodations.

Alboquerque had met with the king of Hormuz. Satisfied, the Portuguese proceeded to Quriyat, which attempted to resist and was subsequently destroyed. Next came Muscat. Having learned the fate of Quriyat, the governor of Muscat immediately offered to submit and supply the Europeans with provisions. When reinforcements arrived from the interior, though, the Muscatis resolved to resist. De Alboquerque had some difficulty subjugating the town, but in the end Muscat fell. The price of their resistance was high: The Portuguese massacred the people, cutting off the ears and noses of those they spared, looted everything of value, and then burned the entire town before proceeding to Sohar. Sohar was at first determined to resist but soon agreed to submit and pay an annual tribute. De Alboquerque spared the city and even appointed an Arab governor to act as Portuguese representative. Khor Fakkan was the final stop, and when its governor failed to offer submission, it suffered the same fate as Muscat. In little more than a month, the Portuguese conquered the entire coast of Oman.

De Alboquerque, after spending a year at Socotra preparing for the final subjugation of Hormuz, next appeared on the Omani coast in August 1508. On this occasion only Qalhat was put to the sword;

Portuguese policy was to allow the Arabs and their Hormuzi overlords a free hand as long as the annual tribute was paid. In 1521 the Portuguese faced a concerted revolt against their control of the Omani coast and throughout the Gulf. The Portuguese garrison at Sohar was massacred, but the agent at Qalhat was able to escape to Muscat, whose Arab governor, a Shaikh Rashid, sided with the Portuguese against the Persian-inspired revolt. With Arab help, the Portuguese regained Sohar, which was then taken from Hormuz, and placed a garrison at Muscat, which became their main trading post replacing Qalhat.

A second challenge to Portuguese authority in Oman came in 1546 when the Ottomans began naval activities in the Gulf and bombarded Muscat. This caused the Portuguese to fortify the town, a process that had only just begun when Piri Pasha took Muscat after a three-week siege in 1552, although he did not remain in control. Then again in 1554 the Ottoman fleet challenged the Portuguese in Omani waters, but after some initial successes, the Turks were routed in August off Fahl Island and never again appeared. Opposition to the Portuguese then started to come from new, more formidable powers: the Dutch, British, and French. Muscat was fortified even more. In 1586-1587 Fort Jalali was built, followed in the next year by Fort Mirani. These forts helped to preserve Portuguese control of Muscat during the Persians invasion in 1623 following their capture of Hormuz. Thereafter, Muscat served as the focus of Portuguese maritime activities: It became the base of the Portuguese fleet and the main port of call for all merchants.

Despite these efforts, Portuguese control of Muscat and the rest of the Omani coast was about to receive its final challenge. In interior Oman, the authority of the Nabahana jabara collapsed in the second decade of the 1600s. A period of chaos followed during which various tribes competed for control of Oman. Tired of fighting, in 1640 the Omanis finally emerged from their long dark age; Nasir b. Murshid al-Ya'aribi was elected imam with the goal of restoring Omani control over all of Oman.

# 3

## Oman's Imperial Age

Throughout most of its medieval history Oman was subjected to a series of foreign invasions and divided by domestic rivalries with competing imams and by long periods of rule by jabara or tyrants. In the seventeenth century that situation had changed as the country was first convulsed by a civil war and then united under the imamate of Nasir b. Murshid al-Ya'aribi. Although Nasir was unable to expel the Portuguese, an honor that fell to his successor, he did begin two centuries in which Oman became the major Asian power in the western Indian Ocean.

Under the Ya'aribah dynasty (1624–1749) and the first century of the Al Bu Sa'id (1749–present) dynasty the Omani fleet challenged Portuguese, Dutch, British, and French merchantmen at sea while extending its authority to the coasts of Iran, the Gulf, and East Africa. By the mid-nineteenth century, though, Omani glory was at an end. Europeans came to control the Indian Ocean trade, and their need for maritime stability prevented the sayyids (title for all members of the Al Bu Sa'id royal family and used by the rulers of Muscat until the mid-nineteenth century) from asserting their control over recalcitrant neighbors. Domestically, the conflict between the religious ideal of the imamate and the reality of commercial empire resulted in still more political turmoil, ending with the reestablishment of an imamate in 1868.

### THE YA'ARIBAH

Nasir b. Murshid al-Ya'aribi was one of the numerous claimants for control of Oman in the early seventeenth century. He had the backing of the religious elite, however, and in 1624 he gained the legitimacy of the imamate in an election that, like so many in Omani history, was not universally recognized. Faced with the opposition of the various warlords, including members of his own family, the new imam had no

Jabrin palace, Oman's most important nonmilitary architectural monument. The residence and religious school were built by Belarab b. Sultan al-Ya'aribi in the 1680s and served as the official residence for several imams. The palace was recently restored by the sultanate's ministry of national heritage and culture.

choice but to fight. Nasir's first efforts were directed toward his home area of the Ghadaf in which he captured Rustaq and Nakhl, but even there the new imam's authority was questioned and he was forced to suppress a revolt before marching his armies onward. Then Nasir added Izki, Nizwa, the Sharqiyah, Sirr, and the Dhahirah (the last with considerable difficulty), followed by Buraimi and most of the coastal lands along the Gulf.

Having thereby secured control of interior Oman, Nasir took on the Portuguese along the coasts. An attack on Muscat was thwarted, but Julfar fell in 1633. A subsequent campaign against Sohar proved disastrous as the Omanis were unable to capture that port, and the Portuguese retaliated by forbidding the Arabs to trade at Muscat. Nasir was forced to negotiate a settlement with the Europeans to restore the much-needed access to Muscat. This did not prevent the imam from assuming control of Quriyat, Sur, and the Ja'lan, thus isolating the Portuguese in Muscat and Sohar. Nasir then had to contend with a serious challenge to his authority in the form of a tribal uprising led by the Bani Hilal. Once that was suppressed, Nasir again turned on the Portuguese. Sohar fell in 1643, but Muscat remained securely in

Portuguese hands. An attack in 1648 almost succeeded in overrunning the port, but Nasir, near death, agreed to a settlement that allowed the Portuguese to retain control of Muscat but turned Matrah over to the Omanis and guaranteed their free trade in Muscat. The imam died in April 1649.

Nasir's successor, Sultan b. Saif al-Ya'aribi I (1649–1679), paid little heed to his uncle's treaty with the Portuguese; immediately upon election as imam he laid plans for their final expulsion from Oman. First the Omani navy was strengthened for a seaborne attack, and in late 1649 the tribes were gathered near Matrah. When the attack on Muscat came, the Portuguese were taken by surprise, probably because Sultan had gathered such a small army. When the Omanis gained entry to the port, the Portuguese commander withdrew to Fort Mirani, but weary after several years fighting and realizing the futility of continued resistance he finally surrendered. Sultan claimed the bulk of the Portuguese fleet harbored at Muscat as booty but allowed the garrison to withdraw to Goa. Oman was united.

Once the Portuguese had been expelled, Sultan carried the war against the infidels to sea, and his successors Balarab b. Sultan (1679–1692) and Saif b. Sultan (1692–1711) continued the policy of imperial expansion. Utilizing the Portuguese ships captured at Muscat and others added later through capture or construction and a mix of Arab, European, and Indian sailors, the Ya'aribah fleet became the scourge of the western Indian Ocean. The Portuguese did prove to be a minor irritant as they continued to cruise the Omani coast, but their half-hearted conduct of the war did not prevent the Omanis from extending their attacks to India and Africa. Diu, Bassain, Bombay, and Surat all were subjected to Omani raids, and in 1655, after a five-year blockade, Mombasa was temporarily occupied by the Ya'aribah. Other Europeans also experienced the onslaught of Ya'aribah "piracies"; English, Dutch, and French merchant shipping in the Indian Ocean and the Gulf was attacked. Persian mercantile interests were so seriously threatened by the Ya'aribah that the Safavids sought European assistance against them. By the end of the seventeenth century the Omani empire extended from East Africa, with Pemba, Zanzibar, Patta, and Kilwa all governed by the Ya'aribah governor at Mombasa, to Bahrain, which was occupied in 1700.

Domestically, the period of the first three Ya'aribah was a time of wealth and stability. Slaves, gold, ivory, hides, and lumber from East Africa, coffee from Yemen, textiles, spices, and rice from India, pearls and copper from the Gulf region, and Oman's own dates, fruit, fish, and horses—all flowed through Muscat, and the Muscati fleet collected a tax from all Arab shipping in the Gulf as protection against pirates. This wealth went into a rash of new building. Sultan b. Saif rebuilt the towns of Birkat al-Mawz and Ibra as well as the distinctive round fort at Nizwa, his capital. The weak Balarab, who eventually committed suicide during the power struggle with his aggressive younger brother Saif, devoted almost his entire attention to the construction of the beautiful palace and school at Jabrin. Saif, who made his capital at Rustaq, was most active in the restoration of the country's falaj systems, especially those in the Batinah, and reportedly came to own a third of the land in Oman.

Ya'aribah fortunes, both literally and figuratively, declined rapidly during the reign of Sultan b. Saif II (1711–1719). The development of empire in East Africa and attacks on India continued, but the new imam drained the treasury with the construction of the last great Ya'aribah building project, the fortress at Hazm. Also by Sultan II's time the religious leaders were beginning to question the suitability of the hereditary, increasingly cosmopolitan, and wealthy Ya'aribah regime. Opposition had first been expressed during the reign of Saif, who at least had had to contend with the Portuguese threat to the Omani coast. Most ulema members were willing to accept dynastic rule in times of military necessity but not when Oman was secure and prosperous. The issue came to a head in 1719 when Sultan died leaving only a minor son.

## CIVIL WAR AND THE AL BU SA'ID IMAMATE, 1719–1785

Serious divisions surfaced at the convocation to elect Sultan's successor. The tribal leaders favored the dead imam's minor son whereas the ulema again compromised its principles by backing another member of the Ya'aribah but one who was at least of age. No decision could be reached; the tribes elected Saif b. Sultan II whereas the ulema elected a rival. As a result the Ya'aribah were divided: In the next five years six elections were held, with Saif II winning three. In 1723 the conflict became a general civil war when Muhammad b. Nasir al-Ghafiri, from the Nizar tribal confederation, entered the fray on behalf of Saif and Khalf b. Mubarak, tamimah of the Bani Hina, a Yamani tribe, sided with the opposition. All Oman's tribes allied themselves with either the Ghafiri or Hinawi, thus initiating the two factions that dominate Omani tribal society to this day. The civil war raged on with Muhammad b. Nasir—who had secured for himself election to the imamate in 1724—controlling the interior and Khalf b. Mubarak exercising authority in Muscat and along the coast. Then in 1728 both Muhammad and Khalf were killed in battle near Sohar. Saif b. Sultan, now an adult, was elected imam yet again.

Plaster work and calligraphy decoration in Jabrin palace. The palace is unique in Oman for its carving, plaster work, and painted decorations.

The Ghafiri, once Saif's supporters, now turned on him and in 1732 secured the election of yet another Ya'aribah imam, Balarab b. Himyar. Saif brought in Huti Baluchi mercenaries from the Makran coast of India to shore up his imamate, but his army was defeated in Sirr. Balarab countered by inviting Persian support. The Persians, hoping no doubt to eliminate the Omani threat in the Gulf, gladly sent an army that landed at Julfar and marched inland. Differences between Balarab and his Persian allies led to the latter's temporary withdrawal, but in 1738 the Persians invaded on their own. Their march through Oman was marked by such outrage against the civilian population that Balarab became completely discredited. He resigned the imamate and joined with Saif, who was besieged in Muscat by the Persians, and helped to expel the invaders.

That was not the end of it. In 1742 the Omanis again rejected Saif in favor of Sultan b. Murshid al-Ya'aribi. This time Saif invited the Persians to come to his assistance. While Sultan besieged Saif in Muscat, the Persian army marched from Julfar to Sohar, where Saif's governor Ahmad b. Sa'id Al Bu Sa'id was able to withstand the siege. The Persians then marched to Muscat, were joined by the Persian fleet, and relieved Saif. Rather than turn the port over to their ally the Persians occupied it themselves. Ahmad b. Sa'id was then driven from Sohar, although he did manage to take the port of Birka.

In 1743 both Sultan b. Murshid and Saif b. Sultan died. Oman was in chaos. Although the Persians held the major ports of Muscat and Sohar, Ahmad b. Sa'id controlled most of the coast and had Hinawi support, and the Ghafiri in the interior elected Balarab b. Himyar al-Ya'aribi imam for a second time. Balarab devoted his efforts to consolidating his position against family rivals and hoping that Ahmad b. Sa'id would wear himself out against the Persians. That was not to be. In 1744 the Persians, anxious to withdraw from Oman, accepted Ahmad b. Sa'id's offer of safe conduct for their return to Iran, an offer that he subsequently reneged on and the Persians were slaughtered. Ahmad's success against the Persians greatly enhanced his reputation. There followed a five-year struggle between Ahmad and Balarab for control of Oman. Ahmad emerged the victor and was elected imam in Nizwa in 1749.

The reign of Ahmad b. Sa'id Al Bu Sa'id (1749–1783)—although it marked the establishment of the dynasty that currently rules Oman—differs little from that of the early Ya'aribah. The imam faced tremendous difficulties: The country had been devastated by civil war and Persian invasions, not all the tribes had accepted his election, commerce was suffering, and the overseas empire had been lost. Ahmad's first task was to suppress tribal opposition with an army of Baluchi mercenaries and African slaves. The imam also dispatched a governor to Zanzibar to reassert Omani control over East Africa and to oversee the collection of the tax on slaves and tribute from the Swahili rulers, who had taken advantage of Oman's long period of troubles to assert their independence. Muscati trading activities in the Gulf were also protected, most notably in 1776 when Ahmad dispatched a fleet to Basra to assist the Ottoman government in ending a blockade of that port by Karim Khan Zand. As a reward, the Ottomans granted a customs waiver at Basra to the Al Bu Sa'id, which served to give the Omanis a virtual monopoly of the coffee trade between Yemen and Iraq. Domestically, Ahmad was most active in encouraging the restoration of Oman's falaj systems. By the imam's death in 1783 the country had regained some of its Ya'aribah glory.

Unfortunately, two problems that had plagued the Ya'aribah continued under the Al Bu Sa'id: family divisions and ulema opposition to hereditary rule. Even before his death, Ahmad b. Sa'id had had to deal with revolts by his younger sons Saif and Sultan. These divisions within the family were only exacerbated when Ahmad secured the election of his son Sa'id as imam, a move that was rejected by Ahmad's other sons, the ulema, who had compromised for too long the ideal of nonhereditary rule, and the tribal leaders, who resented Al Bu Sa'id domination. The end began when Qais b. Ahmad seized Sohar. Hamad b. Sa'id, the imam's son, was able to defeat revolts by two other uncles, Saif and Sultan, and a tribal uprising in Jawf. However, then he too rejected his father's rule, took control of Muscat, and established an independent state claiming neither the spiritual authority of the imamate— a meaningless title that was left to his father in Rustaq—nor temporal power in Oman, which fell to the fissiparous tribes in the interior. Instead, Hamad sought to build a commercial empire in the Indian Ocean with Muscat as its hub.

## THE SAYYIDS OF MUSCAT, 1785–1829

In 1785 the trade in the Gulf was depressed owing to the death of Karim Khan Zand in Persia, European conflict in the Gulf, and recurrent plague in Iraq. This created a vacuum as the major traders had little interest in an area of marginal commercial importance. Hamad sought to fill that vacuum by encouraging trade to come to Muscat and by preventing the emergence of rivals. Customs duties at Muscat were regularized at 6.5 percent, commercial contacts were initiated with the Indus valley, and Tippu Sultan, the ruler of Mysore and himself very interested in commercial expansion, was permitted to open a trading post at Muscat. Sayyid Hamad also attempted to assert Muscati control over the Straits of Hormuz by enlarging his navy and occupying the ports of Khor Fakkan and Jazirat al-Hamra. These actions were successful, and by 1792 Muscat had become the main entrepôt of the Gulf.

Hamad's death disrupted Muscat's commercial development for a time as Imam Sa'id tried to reassert his control over the port but was challenged by Qais b. Ahmad of Sohar and Sultan b. Ahmad, who had been living in exile at Gwadur on the Makran coast but returned to Oman on Hamad's death to seize Birka and march on Muscat. After a brief blockade, Muscat was captured and Oman formally divided with the Pact of Birka in 1793, which recognized Sa'id's authority in Rustaq, Qais' in Sohar, and Sultan's in Muscat.

### Sultan b. Ahmad

Sultan b. Ahmad (1792–1804) clearly dominated Omani affairs for the next decade and rates as one of his country's greatest rulers. Like Hamad, Sultan ignored the tribes and devoted his efforts to overseas expansion. His first concern was to reassert Muscat's control over the southern Gulf where both Khor Fakkan and Jazirat al-Hamra had been lost to the Qawasim of Ras al-Khaimah. Sultan, who already possessed the port of Gwadur on the Makran coast, by virtue of an agreement with the Khan of Kalat, seized Chahbar on the Persian coast and then in 1798, after a brief military campaign, obtained the customs farm for Bandar Abbas, which included the islands of Hormuz, Qishm, Hanjam, and Minab. This gave Sultan access to the markets of southern Persia, which his agents quickly developed, secured control of the Straits of Hormuz, and gave him the valuable salt deposits of Hormuz. The sayyid then instituted a 2.5 percent levy on all native shipping entering the Gulf, ostensibly to be used to finance protection against pirates, and began working closely with several Gulf pirates to ensure that the tax would be paid.

Sultan's chief concern was that rival Gulf merchants would begin direct trade with India and thus bypass Muscat or Bandar Abbas. The Utub, who had occupied the island of Bahrain in 1783, were the main threat, and the sayyid launched his first campaign against them in 1799. In the next year the Utub agreed to terms whereby they would pay Sultan's transit tax and a tribute equal to half the amount that they had previously paid to Persia. When the Utub were less than diligent in sending the 1801 remittance, Sultan again attacked the island. However, by this time the Bahrainis had found themselves a powerful ally in the Saudis.

The Saudis made their first appearance in Oman in 1799 when they occupied the Buraimi oasis. By 1800 they had become a sufficient threat to Muscati commercial interests, mostly through their domination

Nizwa Fort. Built during the reign of Saif b. Sultan al-Ya'aribi, the round tower fort at Nizwa is Oman's most distinctive example of military architecture.

of the Qawasim, that Sultan allied with his brother Qais in Sohar and marched to Buraimi to expel the invaders. The campaign was a failure, and faced with certain retribution, Sultan agreed to pay an annual tribute to the Saudi amir and to allow a Saudi garrison and agent to be placed in Muscat. Despite the treaty, Sultan continued to work against the Saudis. An attempted alliance with the sherif of Mecca in 1803 failed, and in retaliation the Saudis backed a coup by Badr b. Saif Al Bu Sa'id in Muscat. Sultan negotiated a new agreement with the Saudis that saved his throne. Later in the year the Saudi amir was assassinated, temporarily removing any new Saudi threat.

Sultan again turned his attention to Gulf affairs. The pasha of Baghdad's failure to remit the customs charges on Omani imports to Basra gave the sayyid cause to sail to that port in late 1804. Despite their disagreement about the customs charges, Sultan and the pasha did take time to discuss a joint Muscati-Ottoman campaign against the Saudis. That campaign never materialized for in November as Sultan approached Qishm on his return voyage to Muscat his ship was attacked by pirates. Rather than flee, Sultan stood and fought. He was killed in the battle.

### Sa'id b. Sultan and Gulf Expansion

Sayyid Sultan's death threw Muscat into the predictable turmoil. Sultan's two young sons, Salim and Sa'id, were incapable of controlling the situation and called on their cousin, Badr b. Saif, the Saudi sympathizer, to assist them. Badr did neutralize any threat from the Saudis, but his attempts to subdue interior Oman (and reportedly to impose Wahabism) came at the expense of Muscat's Gulf interests. All the Gulf islands fell to the Qawasim, who became a formidable naval power. Then in March 1806 Badr's brief reign came to an end when he was assassinated by the new ruler of Muscat, Sayyid Sa'id b. Sultan. The new sayyid's immediate concerns were domestic. First, he assured the Saudis that he intended to continue to pay the annual tribute and maintain friendly relations. He then removed the main threat within the Al Bu Said family by taking control of Sohar from Azzan b. Qais in 1807. Oman secured, Sa'id turned his attention to the Gulf.

Muscati authority in the Gulf had dwindled to practically nil in the three years since Sayyid Sultan's death. Sa'id did regain the port of Chahbar and the island dependencies of Bandar Abbas but met with far less success elsewhere. The Saudis remained a threat. Sa'id's policy was to ignore their activities in Oman, where resistance was left to the tribes, while attacking them elsewhere in the Gulf. Sa'id was helped immeasurably when Muhammad Ali of Egypt invaded the peninsula in 1811. Bahrain was another challenge. The Utub were rapidly becoming the most successful merchants in the Gulf. Like his father, Sa'id had only limited successes against them—most notably the occupation of Bahrain in 1811—but the tribe was remarkably adept at negotiating settlements that acknowledged Muscati hegemony and promised the payment of tribute that were forgotten as soon as the sayyid's fleet sailed over the horizon.

But the main challenge to Muscat came from the Qawasim of Ras al-Khaima. This tribe, inhabiting both sides of the Gulf, had become notorious brigands, preying upon all shipping often with grisly results. During Sultan's times the Qawasim threat had actually benefited Muscat because the sayyid had been powerful enough to control, or at least protect against, their activities. That was no longer the case. Sa'id made several attempts to eliminate the Qawasim. An attack on the port of Khor Fakkan failed in 1808 as did one later in the year on Ras al-Khaimah. In 1809 Sa'id joined with a British expedition against Ras al-Khaimah, but it too was unsuccessful as the Saudis intervened and the British did not wish to involve themselves in a conflict with them. In 1813 Sa'id tried to take advantage of a rivalry within the Qawasim ruling family by supporting a rival shaikhdom in Sharjah. The results were not what he had expected: In 1815 the Qawasim burst out of the Gulf, attacked Omani shipping between India and Ras al-Hadd, and even bombarded Matrah. After yet more unsuccessful attempts to conquer Bahrain and Ras al-Khaimah, Sa'id was faced with a hopeless situation and turned to the British for help.

By 1819 the Qawasim, sometimes supported by the Saudis, had become the scourge of the Gulf, threatening not only Muscati shipping but all commerce from India to Africa to the Gulf. The British, determined to end this threat to their merchants, started to search for allies. Both Sayyid Sa'id and Muhammad Ali were approached. Sa'id was reluctant to participate in any venture that included the Egyptians as he perceived them to be a greater threat to his interests than the Qawasim. When Muhammad Ali declined to join the expedition, though, Sa'id was more than happy to assist the British. Accordingly, in December 1819 a Muscati-British fleet bombarded Ras al-Khaimah, and the Qawasim were defeated.

Sa'id's expectations undoubtedly were that Ras al-Khaimah would be turned over to him and that the British would help him to subjugate Bahrain, which he depicted to his allies as another nest of pirates. Instead, the British, who had considered giving Ras al-Khaimah to Sa'id, concluded a treaty with the Qawasim and the other tribes along the coast that in effect recognized their independence and ended naval warfare in the Gulf. Then the British not only refused to assist Sa'id

Nizwa street scene. The old capital of the imamate, Nizwa is a well-preserved example of traditional Oman. Its large houses, which abut narrow streets, provide much-needed shade. Walled gardens, often protected by defensive towers, lie within the city limits. Gates divide the various quarters of the city.

against the Utub but admitted that tribe to their trucial system and advised the sayyid strongly against attacking Bahrain.

### Sa'id and East Africa

With Gulf expansion seemingly closed to him, Sa'id turned his attention to another area of Omani interest—East Africa. The Swahili coast had been largely ignored by the Al Bu Sa'id although the sayyids had collected a head tax on exported slaves. Control was minimal and direct intervention rare; Ahmad b. Sa'id had dispatched a governor to Zanzibar and Sa'id b. Sultan had conducted a brief military campaign there in 1812. Muscat's principal adversaries on the coast were the Mazru'i of Mombasa, who had proclaimed their independence of Oman in 1814. In 1820 Sa'id took two actions designed to assert Muscati authority in East Africa. First, the fleet was sent to the Somali coast to conquer Mogadishu and some neighboring smaller ports. Then Sa'id planned an attack on the Bani Bu Ali tribe of Ja'lan.

The Bani Bu Ali expedition is a unique event in Sa'id's reign: It is the only time that the sayyid conducted a land campaign against an Omani tribe. The Bani Bu Ali were a powerful independent tribe with few maritime interests but virtual control over the ports of Sur and al-Ashkara. They, therefore, were potential rivals to any interests that Sa'id might have in East Africa. Since Sa'id did not have the resources to launch a campaign, he convinced the British that the tribe had committed acts of piracy and was able thus to gain their help. The first attack on the town of Bilad Bani Bu Ali failed miserably, but the affront to the British military served only to strengthen British resolve to defeat the tribe, although everyone realized that the war served only Sa'id's interests. The second attack was successful, but the British were appalled by Sa'id's treatment of his enemy as he destroyed their homes, cut down palm trees, ruined aflaj, and requested that all adult males of the tribe be imprisoned in Bombay. The Bani Bu Ali were no longer a threat to Sa'id.

During the next two years Sa'id devoted his attentions to East Africa. In 1821-1822 several Swahili ports were attacked, conquered, and garrisoned with Muscati troops. These gains were consolidated during the following year so that Mombasa and the Mazru'i were surrounded. An unsuccessful siege of the town in 1823 was followed by the declaration of a British protectorate in February 1824 by William Owen, a British naval commander on a mission for the governor of Mauritius to suppress the slave trade, who had received a promise from the Mazru'i they would stop exporting slaves. Sa'id perceived the protectorate as a threat equal to the maritime truces in the Gulf and immediately began a diplomatic effort in Bombay and London to secure its end. Despite repeated assurances from the British that the protectorate had not been sanctioned by the British government and that it would be eliminated, not until 1826 was Sa'id again free to take action.

The interregnum caused by Owen's protectorate did result in Sa'id's involving himself in Gulf affairs once again as he renegotiated the contract for Bandar Abbas, concluded a marriage alliance with the Persian government, secured Muscat's preferential treatment at Basra, and made threatening noises against Bahrain. Once Owens withdrew from Mombasa, though, Sa'id's sights again shifted to East Africa. After an attempt at a negotiated settlement with the Mazru'i failed in 1827, Sa'id himself sailed to the Swahili coast, defeated the Mazru'i, and garrisoned Mombasa. No sooner had the sayyid set sail for Muscat than the Mazru'i revolted and expelled the garrison. Meanwhile, Sa'id, still dreaming of an empire stretching from Basra to Madagascar, planned yet another attack on Bahrain. It too failed, and Sa'id had to be content with a treaty with the Utub recognizing the independence of Bahrain and promising help in defending the island if attacked.

By 1828 Sa'id was faced with difficult circumstances. Muscat's once dominant position in the Gulf had eroded irretrievably as the Utub and Qawasim, both virtual British protectorates, carried more and more of the trade with India. In East Africa Muscati control was tenuous as Mazru'i independence threatened control of trade in that region. In 1829 Sa'id decided to focus all his attentions on East Africa and to make Zanzibar the hub of a new commercial empire with plantation agriculture as its basis. Muscat was to have only a secondary role in the new economic order.

## OMANI DISSATISFACTION, 1829–1868

Oman had been of little concern to Sa'id during the first twenty years of his reign, but for the remainder the country was to be a constant irritant because in attempting to secure Muscat for his regents while he remained in Zanzibar the sayyid began interfering in Omani politics. The main threat to Sa'id's absentee control of Muscat was his own family. Accordingly, Sa'id violated a safe conduct pass and imprisoned the very popular ruler of Suwayq, Hilal b. Muhammad Al Bu Sa'id, just before setting sail for Zanzibar in 1829. The result was a revolt in 1830 in which Hilal's cause was supported by Hamud b. Azzan Al Bu Sa'id, the ruler of Rustaq, whose father had been expelled by Sa'id from Sohar. When Hamud seized Sohar and other Batinah ports, the sayyid's governor in Muscat rapidly sought Sa'id's return.

Meanwhile, Sa'id had occupied Dhofar and added it to the Muscati empire when en route to Zanzibar. This area had been under the

Garden tower. Such towers offer protection against attacks and sometimes guard wells.

authority of Muhammad b. Aqil, a notorious Red Sea pirate, who had established himself in Salalah in 1804 and ruled until his assassination by the Qara in 1829. Sa'id did not place a garrison in Dhofar, which seems to have fallen into a state of anarchy with constant warfare between the Qara and Kathiri. Control in Salalah passed to an interesting character named Muhammad Lorleyd who was reportedly an American who had survived one of Muhammad b. Aqil's attacks on a U.S. ship and been raised by the pirate.

When Sa'id returned to Muscat in late spring 1830 the situation in Oman had stabilized. Hilal was released from prison and restored to Suwayq, but Hamud could not be budged from Sohar. Sa'id accepted the status quo and left for Zanzibar in 1832. Hamud and Hilal again joined forces and attacked Rustaq. Further, the Qawasim occupied Khor Fakkan and Dibbah on the Shimiliyah coast. Sa'id rushed back to Muscat. The pattern continued. Sa'id was able to negotiate a settlement with Hamud that left him in control of Sohar, but as soon as Sa'id left, Hamud would attack. By the end of the decade, Hamud b. Azzan became the focus of those dissatisfied with the sultans of Muscat, along with the Al Bu Sa'id of Muscat, who no longer had the funds to support prosperity throughout Oman. Tribal leaders even considered bestowing the imamate on Hamud. Hamud's imprisonment and eventual death in a Muscati jail in 1849 only aggravated the situation by further alienating the tribes from Sa'id. Hamud's brother Qais became Oman's new hope. Sa'id's support in Oman was also not helped by his alliance with the Saudis, especially when his son Thuwaini, the governor of Muscat, used Saudi troops to compel the tribes of the Batinah to pay their taxes. Despite these problems, Sa'id had sufficient power to expel Qais from Sohar and appoint his son Turki governor.

### Thuwaini b. Sa'id and Oman

Sa'id b. Sultan's death in 1856, while en route to Zanzibar, meant very little for Oman. Qais b. Azzan controlled Rustaq; Turki b. Sa'id Sohar, the tribes in the rest of Oman; and Thuwaini b. Sa'id, only Muscat. Thuwaini's main concern, however, was Zanzibar, where another brother, Majid, had assumed the throne. Thuwaini asserted his rights to all of Sa'id's territories but in subsequent negotiations with Majid renounced any claim to Zanzibar in exchange for an annual payment of MT$40,000 (MT dollar, which stands for Maria Theresa dollar, is an Austrian coin used from the late eighteenth century to the 1960s as Oman's principal currency). Majid did not continue the payments, however, and Thuwaini was eventually forced to accept British mediation in the dispute. In April 1861 Muscat and Zanzibar were declared independent sultanates with the latter paying MT$40,000 a year in compensation to the former.

With his hopes of empire dashed, Thuwaini turned his attentions to Oman. The sultan seized Sohar from his brother in the summer of 1861, after imprisoning Turki during a British-sponsored peace conference. Later in the year, Thuwaini faced a major uprising led by Qais b. Azzan and the Al-Sa'd of the Batinah. Although Qais b. Azzan was killed in the uprising, the rebels held firm under Azzan b. Qais until they were eventually forced to withdraw to Rustaq. Thuwaini was on the verge of defeating Azzan in Rustaq when Azzan called on the Saudis for assistance.

Saudi intervention almost resulted in Thuwaini's gaining control of all Oman. After relieving Azzan in Rustaq, the Saudi force proceeded to Ja'lan, joined with the Bani Bu Ali, and occupied Sur in August 1865. The murder of a Hindu merchant there brought British involvement. Gunboats sent to the Gulf bombarded Saudi ports, and Thuwaini was not only encouraged to take a more active role against the Saudis but given the wherewithal to do so. The British gave him artillery and, more important, ensured that Sultan Majid paid the Zanzibar subsidy, including arrears. Thuwaini, with plenty of money, then received support from Salih b. Ali, the tamimah of the Hirth, who gathered a force of Hinawi tribespeople to help the sultan, as well as from his brother Turki. In January 1866 Thuwaini and his Omani allies gathered at Sohar for an attack on Buraimi, the Saudi headquarters. Then, at the peak of his authority in Oman, the sultan was assassinated by his son Salim and a Wahabi accomplice.

### A New Regime

Despite the patricide, Salim b. Thuwaini was recognized as sultan. His reputation as a conservative Ibadi brought him the support of the main cleric, Sa'id b. Khalfan al-Khalili, and the continued backing of Salih b. Ali. Turki b. Sa'id refused to support his nephew and was arrested for a time; he then was released at the insistence of the British and raised an army with which to overthrow Salim. He was almost successful in the summer of 1867 but was prevented from taking Muscat by the British. Salim, buoyed by this show of British support, overextended his position by seeking to imprison Salih b. Ali while he was visiting Muscat. Salih escaped to Rustaq and the safety of Azzan b. Qais before returning to the Sharqiyah to gather his troops for an attack on Muscat in retaliation. Sa'id b. Khalfan al-Khalili and Azzan b. Qais quickly joined the revolt. In September 1868 Azzan marched down the Batinah and joined with Salih b. Ali outside Muscat. Salim was invited to repent his evil ways and accept the guidance of the ulema. The sultan, anticipating British and Ghafiri tribal support, refused. On October 1 Muscat fell to the rebel forces. Salim, vainly awaiting the gunboats from India, held out in one of Muscat's forts until October 12 when he finally left Oman.

For two hundred years between 1624 and 1856 Oman was an international power with territorial control extending to the Gulf and the east coast of Africa. By the 1830s domestic pressures threatened that position. With the death of Sayyid Sa'id in 1856 those domestic pressures erupted as Oman was convulsed by prolonged, low-level civil war. In 1868 conservative forces succeeded in expelling the Al Bu Sa'id from Oman and instituting a new regime that, although it did not retain control of Muscat for very long, did mark the beginning of a new era in Omani history.

# 4

# *Imamate and Sultanate*

Salim b. Thuwaini's expulsion from Muscat by Ibadi tribespeople desiring a theocratic imamate initiated a new era in Omani history: For the next century the Al Bu Sa'id dynasty of Muscat found itself involved in a struggle for survival not just in Oman but also in Muscat. Oman and Muscat, effectively divided politically in 1785, drifted further and further apart as the tribes of the interior began electing imams to govern their affairs whereas the sultans of Muscat, dominated by the British, controlled the coast. This political situation was formalized in 1920 with the Treaty of Sib and did not end until 1954 when Oman was reunited by Sultan Sa'id b. Taimur.

## THE IMAMATE OF AZZAN B. QAIS

Once the Ibadi tribespeople had consolidated their hold over Muscat, the city's new leaders sought to implement the ideal of an imam ruling over the perfect Islamic state. A committee of religious and tribal leaders, dominated by Sa'id b. Khalfan al-Khalili and Salih b. Ali al-Hirthi, was convened; it nominated Azzan b. Qais Al Bu Sa'id and presented him for public approval. Recognition was granted with the condition that the imam seek the advice of the religious leaders before taking major actions. Al-Khalili, as governor of Muscat and chief qadi, became Azzan's main adviser, and al-Khalili's followers, the white-turbaned religious idealists known as *mutawwi's*, enforced the shaikh's every wish. Imam Azzan dealt exclusively with military affairs, counting on the support of moderate tribes like the Hirth and Yal-Sa'd.

Azzan's pacification of Oman occurred rapidly. The principal opposition came from the Ghafiri tribes of Jabal al-Akhdar, Dhahirah, and the Jawf, which had remained neutral in the conflict between Azzan and Salim b. Thuwaini. In winter and spring 1869 the Wadi Sama'il and Ja'lan regions were pacified by the imam, and in June the Saudis were expelled from Buraimi. After resting for the summer, Azzan marched

53

Bawshar. The village of Bawshar, 20 miles (35 km) from Muscat, is a typical Omani agricultural settlement. It is situated against the mountains, and water is available in wells within the gravels of the wadi and in the aflaj that tap into surrounding sources. The houses are built among the date palms.

into the Jawf and in October captured the fort at Nizwa, thereby ending resistance in the Omani heartland. The last Ghafiri stronghold, Hazm fort, fell in November. Finally, the Bani Riyam, following the arrest and imprisonment of Shaikh Saif b. Sulaiman while under a safe-conduct pass to Muscat, submitted to the imam. For the first time in almost a century, Oman was united under a single ruler.

Azzan's means of pacification proved to be his undoing. The Hinawi remained active supporters of the imamate, but the Ghafiri were only alienated further by the imam's harsh military measures and the treachery against the Riyam and other tribes. Al-Khalili's activities in Muscat also caused trouble. Customs revenues fell dramatically because of the shaikh's hostile attitude toward Muscat's large and commercially important Hindu community. The government began a series of confiscations, first of the property of supporters of the sultanate and then even from the allies of the imamate. Then money was demanded from the tribes and payments to tribal levies halted.

Through the winter of 1870-1871 the position of the imamate eroded. The Ghafiri tribes revolted, and even the Hinawi tribes of the Sharqiyah and Ja'lan, Salih b. Ali's territory, were disgruntled. To add to these difficulties, the Saudis threatened an invasion. Then in September 1870 Turki b. Sa'id Al Bu Sa'id, with financial backing from Zanzibar, landed in Oman and began gathering allies. After defeating Azzan at Dhank in Sirr, Turki quickly took control of Dhahirah, Jawf, and Ja'lan, benefiting greatly by the support of Saif b. Sulaiman and the Bani Riyam.

Turki was prepared for the final assault on the imamate. In January 1871 he divided his army, sending half, under Saif b. Sulaiman, along the coast against Muscat while he attacked Salih b. Ali in Sharqiyah. Saif b. Sulaiman easily took Quriyat and then bypassed Muscat to seize Matrah. Azzan tried to defend that port but on January 30 was killed, along with Saif b. Sulaiman; Turki's supporters were victorious. Al-Khalili sought to hold out in Muscat by barricading himself in one of the forts, but when he was promised protection if he would surrender and withdraw to Sama'il, Muscat was formally turned over to Turki. Turki immediately had Al-Khalili and his son arrested and imprisoned in Fort Jalali, where they were both murdered three months later.

## RESTORATION OF THE SULTANATE

Turki b. Sa'id was only thirty years old when he became sultan in 1871, but he had already led an eventful life. He had been appointed governor of Sohar while still in his teens, revolted against his brother Thuwaini and nephew Salim, been imprisoned on several occasions, lived in exile in Bombay, and plotted and executed the overthrow of the imamate. Turki's victory had been only partial—he directly controlled only Muscat. The rest of the country was divided among Salih b. Ali al-Hirthi in the Sharqiyah, Ibrahim b. Qais Al Bu Sa'id, the imam's brother, in Sohar and the Batinah, the Saudis who had reoccupied Buraimi, and a host of tribal leaders whose loyalty was dependent on the sultan's generosity. Turki had nothing with which to be generous. He also had his own relatives to contend with as Salim b. Thuwaini was seeking to raise support in Ja'lan and Turki's own brother Abd al-Aziz b. Sa'id was in Gwadur planning an assault on Muscat.

### Turki b. Sa'id

Turki's first goals was to establish control over the Batinah. A campaign against Ibrahim b. Qais in summer 1871 accomplished little but a formal recognition of the sultan's rival's authority as far as Khaburah. A severe shortage of funds prevented Turki from doing anything for the next year, but in 1873 he received a windfall when the British agreed not only to pay the Zanzibar subsidy for that year but also to pay it in arrears to 1871. Turki immediately spent most of the money to purchase the loyalty of tribal leaders and to remove Ibrahim b. Qais from Sohar in July 1873. However, the sultan suffered a stroke that nearly killed him and left him physically and mentally disabled for the rest of his life. Ibrahim b. Qais, who had retired to Rustaq, and Salih b. Ali sought to take advantage of the situation. In January 1874 Salih occupied and looted Matrah and threatened to take Muscat before withdrawing after Turki paid him for the insult. In March Ibrahim b. Qais, with the support of the Yal Sa'd, led an uprising in the Batinah that required British intervention. Later in the year the sultan sought to play an active role in mediating tribal disputes in the interior, in an effort to ensure his support among the Ghafiri, but even that failed as his incompetence served only to alienate his allies.

By 1875 Turki was a tired, ill, poor, and bitter man who expressed to the British his desire to abdicate. Instead, they convinced him to take an extended vacation and to leave the affairs of Muscat in the hands of a regent. The choice for the regency was his brother Abd al-Aziz. Abd al-Aziz was an ambitious individual who had more than once sought to obtain the sultanate for himself. He was known to be religiously conservative and may even have aspired to the imamate. Furthermore, he and Turki did not like each other. Turki sailed to Gwadur in August, and Abd al-Aziz immediately undertook actions designed to ensure his becoming sultan, including making overtures to Salih b. Ali. He almost managed to stage a coup; when Turki returned to Muscat in December

Jabrin. This small agricultural village has a typical arrangement of houses and gardens.

he had to retake his capital by force. Abd al-Aziz fled to the Sharqiyah and the protection of Salih b. Ali.

Turki's situation had improved little. By 1877 the Hinawi were again allied against him, and Salih b. Ali was preparing for an assault on Muscat. His forces were joined by those of Ibrahim b. Qais, and it looked as if the Al Bu Sa'id would be expelled from Muscat yet again. A British warship shelled the rebels, and disheartened tribespeople, who had not anticipated such resistance, began to drift away from Salih and Ibrahim's camp. Losing supporters rapidly, Salih quietly withdrew to the Sharqiyah, his reputation severely damaged. Thereafter, Turki lived in relative calm; his peace was only disturbed by one other failed attack by Salih b. Ali on Muscat in 1883. Salih b. Ali and Ibrahim b. Qais had become divided, and both were weary.

The one notable success of Turki's reign was the establishment of direct control over Dhofar. Contacts between Dhofar and Muscat were minimal after Sa'id b. Sultan's temporary occupation of Salalah in 1829, although the Al Bu Sa'id sultans continued to claim authority within the region and reportedly had received delegations from there offering allegiance. That situation was challenged in summer 1876 when Turki received a letter from one Sayyid Fadhl b. Alawi al-Husaini, who claimed to be the ruler of Dhofar on behalf of the Ottomans. Fadhl b. Alawi is another intriguing character that figured prominently in Dhofari history. Fadhl was a Moplah, a descendant of Hadrami Arabs who had settled on the Malabar coast of India and married Indian women. He had developed a reputation as a holy man and claimed descent from the Prophet Muhammad; he then became a political activist, leading to his expulsion from India in 1852. After living for a time in Mecca, Fadhl had settled in Salalah where he had eventually gained the support of the Mahra, Qara, and some Al-Kathir.

By 1878 Fadhl's hold on Dhofar began to slip. The construction of a fort in Salalah and the diligent collection of taxes angered the Qara, who tried to overthrow him. Fadhl sought allies in Yemen and the Hejaz but to no avail. Then in 1879, with encouragement and support from Sultan Turki, the Bait Kathir revolted and expelled Fadhl. Turki immediately sent a *wali* (governor), Sulaiman b. Suwailam, to ensure Muscati control over the province. That control did not come easily: Sulaiman b. Suwailam faced a series of revolts, both on the part of the Al-Kathir, who desired independence of Muscat, and of supporters of Fadhl b. Alawi, which resulted in the expulsion of the Omanis from Salalah in 1885. Control was reestablished in early 1888 when Turki sent his son Faisal with a large force to reinstall Sulaiman b. Suwailam as governor.

### Faisal b. Turki

When Sultan Turki died later in the year, his son Faisal (1888–1913) became the first Al Bu Sa'id ruler of the nineteenth century to assume power peacefully. Faisal b. Turki was twenty-four years old, inexperienced, and ambitious. He wanted to be sultan of all Oman, perhaps even imam, and independent of British interference. His first act was to court conservative support, and his large payments to Salih b. Ali bought at least the neutrality if not outright loyalty of that important tribal leader. Faisal next attempted to overthrow his rival Ibrahim b. Azzan in Rustaq. The campaign was a failure: Faisal's army not only was unable to capture the town, but the Yal Sa'd on the Batinah revolted, thereby adding to Faisal's military difficulties. Then the sultan ran out of money. The blow of Faisal's reputation served to encourage ambitious relatives, such as Abd al-Aziz b. Sa'id and Sa'ud b. Azzan b. Qais Al Bu Sa'id to ally in an effort to overthrow him. Faisal's army spent a year chasing the rebels around Oman.

By 1890 Faisal was demoralized and determined to ignore completely the affairs of Oman, going so far as to refuse to mediate tribal disputes— a major source of prestige and authority for the sultanate—for five years. This policy was equally disastrous; the tribes of the interior fell into anarchy, especially in the strategically and commercially important Wadi

Sama'il where tribal warfare prevented dates from reaching Muscat for export. Faisal's one venture into interior politics almost lost him the sultanate: In late 1894 he conspired to have Salih b. Ali removed as tamimah of the Hirth. Salih learned of the plot and, bolstered by generous aid from the sulṭan of Zanzibar, gathered his well-armed tribespeople to overthrow Muscat. In February 1895 Salih's forces captured the port and raised the white flag of the imamate while Faisal fled to the forts. However, Salih soon found himself besieged in Muscat as Faisal was able to buy the loyalty of the Ghafiri. In March Salih agreed to leave Muscat but only after receiving a pardon and a large payment. Faisal, his lesson learned, again withdrew from Omani politics and spent his time improving Muscat's defences, bickering with the British, and dealing with Dhofari affairs.

The early years of Faisal's reign had been peaceful in Dhofar, and the sultan had been able to garner the support of Shaikh Awadh b. Azzan al-Shanfari of the Al-Kathir and most of the Qara of the Salalah plain. However, opposition to Al Bu Sa'id rule in general and to Wali Sulaiman b. Suwailam in particular was acute. In November 1895 there was a general uprising during which the Muscati garrison was expelled from Salalah and the Al Bu Sa'id was left in control of only Mirbat. The revolt was not suppressed until April 1897. Sulaiman b. Suwailam resumed his position as wali for a brief time but was eventually replaced by a more acceptable individual.

While Sultan Faisal quarreled with his British protectors and barricaded himself in Muscat, a series of very significant changes were taking place in the interior as Salih b. Ali's death in 1896 and that of Ibrahim b. Qais in 1898 paved the way for a new generation of religious and tribal leaders. Sa'ud b. Azzan b. Qais Al Bu Sa'id tried in 1898 to get himself elected imam, but his murder in 1899 removed the last vestiges of the 1868 imamate and ended the Al Bu Sa'id role in the conservative movement. Tribal support came from Isa b. Salih al-Hirthi, who had succeeded his father as tamimah of the Hirth and leader of the Hinawi tribes, and Himyar b. Nasir al-Nabhani, tamimah of the Ghafiri Bani Riyam, a tribe that had become alienated by British efforts to end the slave trade and arms trade through Muscat. Ideological support was provided by a blind theologian, Abdallah b. Humaid al-Salimi. In May 1913 the conservative leadership, excluding Isa b. Salih, convened at Tanuf and elected Salim b. Rashid al-Kharusi, a Ghafiri, as imam and announced the deposing of Sultan Faisal.

## IMAMATE AND SULTANATE

The imamate immediately went on the offensive. Riyami and Hinawi Bani Hina tribal levies quickly captured Nizwa, a success that brought

Typical village house. Most village houses in Oman are connected to each other, with a low wall (upper left) dividing neighboring dwellings. This house contains several large rooms around the courtyard, including separate women's and men's quarters, storage rooms, and a cooking room.

the support of the principal interior tribes and encouraged Isa b. Salih to take an active role. Sultan Faisal sought to raise allies to defend his position. Faisal's own tribal supporters, primarily Sunni Bani Bu Ali from Ja'lan, were sent to Sama'il, his main garrison in the interior, but these were completely surrounded and eventually fled. The towns in the Ghadaf fell easily to the imam's forces. In July the British landed troops to defend Muscat and repeated a warning first issued to the tribes in 1895 that they would not permit the fall of the sultan's capital. In the midst of the conflict, Faisal became ill and died in October and was succeeded by his son Taimur (1913–1931).

### Taimur b. Faisal and Isa b. Salih

Taimur sought to assuage the dissatisfied tribespeople by promising reforms to wipe out social and governmental corruption and by attempting to negotiate with his boyhood acquaintance Isa b. Salih but to no avail. Although a moderate, Isa realized that support for the imamate was strong. He did meet with the sultan in December 1914, but nothing was accomplished. During that year the Batinah was captured by the imamate, and British bombardment was required for Taimur to retain control over Birka and Quriyat. Then in January 1915 the long-anticipated assault on Muscat by the imam came. It failed miserably as the British Indian troops easily defeated the tribal levies.

The sultan's forces staged a brief offensive that regained control over most of the coast and the Ghadaf as the army of the imam withdrew to the interior. Taimur had hoped to extend his authority at least to Sama'il but was dissuaded by the British, who recommended that he accept some kind of political settlement. The sultan's peace overtures to the imam were interpreted as a sign of weakness, and the conservatives demanded a strict enforcement of the sharia, resumption of free arms trade, and Taimur's recognition of the imam's spiritual authority within Oman. Negotiations began at Sib in fall 1915 between Isa b. Salih, representing the imam, and Major George Benn, the British political agent, as the sultan's delegate. These talks came to nothing.

For the next several years the imam consolidated his position in Jawf and retook the Ghadaf, capturing Rustaq in August 1917, while the sultan, at British insistence, reformed his administration. Negotiations were resumed in September 1919 with Ronald Wingate handling the talks for Taimur and Isa b. Salih again representing the imam. Both sides generally wanted to maintain the status quo—the imam ruling the interior and the sultan the coast. The major roadblock to a settlement was the imam's confiscation in 1913 of some gardens owned by members of the royal family in Wadi Ma'awal. The imam, at the insistence of some prominent ulema who were profiting from the confiscated gardens, refused to return them. In retaliation the sultan broke off negotiations and imposed a punitive tax on all Omani produce entering his territory for export. This move hurt, and the imam's intransigence began to alienate many of his followers.

Hope for a settlement improved in April 1920 when Himyar b. Nasir, who reportedly had taken over some of the confiscated gardens, died and was succeeded by his young, inexperienced son Sulaiman. Then in July Imam Salim b. Rashid was assassinated by some Wahiba tribespeople, apparently as a result of their anger over Taimur's punitive tax. The death of the two most powerful conservative ideologues provided the means for the moderate and pragmatic Isa b. Salih to dominate imamate affairs. Muhammad b. Abdallah al-Khalili, tamimah of the Hinawi Bani Ruwahah and Isa's son-in-law, was elected imam and immediately sought to reach an accommodation with the sultan. The disputed gardens were exchanged for four prisoners held by Taimur in a face-saving solution that permitted the new imam to end that roadblock. Isa and Wingate then reopened their negotiations at Sib in September 1920 and quickly reached an agreement. The so-called Treaty of Sib— actually identical letters sent by Isa and the sultan to the political agent—set the basis for relations between Oman and Muscat for the next thirty-five years. Both sides promised not to interfere in each other's affairs and to allow free trade and travel and an exchange of fugitives. Taimur removed the punitive zakat, and Oman was at peace.

In Muscat, Sultan Taimur, whose reign had started under a cloud that he never seemed able to shake, sought only to escape the sultanate. The British forbade him to take extended vacations in India and ignored the sultan's pleadings that he be permitted to abdicate. He began to spend as much time as possible in Dhofar, leaving the administration of the country to a new council of ministers established under a British adviser, and a levy corps under British officers provided the little protection that Muscat required.

The Muscati government did face a series of challenges to its authority. In late 1920 the Yal-Sa'd, the principal tribe of the Batinah, staged an uprising in protest to efforts to establish a customs house at Musna'a. Not until November 1922 did the Muscat levy corps and British gunboats force compliance with the new order. In the south, the Janaba and Bani Bu Ali also resisted attempts to establish a customs house at Sur. The Janaba were sufficiently impressed by a British gunboat to end their opposition, but the Bani Bu Ali were a more serious problem. In 1923 their shaikh, Muhammad b. Nasir, proclaimed himself amir of the Ja'lan, raised his own flag, and started issuing passports. When he opened his own customs house in Sur, the British shelled it. When Muhammad died in 1929 there was some reconciliation between the Muscati government and his successor Ali b. Abdallah, who at least promised to stop flying his flag and issuing passports, but a threat of an aerial bombardment of Bilad Bani Bu Ali in 1932 was required to get him to accept Muscati authority. Another difficulty arose from the Bani Hadiya section of the Shihuh in Ru'us al-Jibal. In 1930 the shaikh of Khasab imprisoned Taimur's wali there and refused to recognize the sultan's authority. Khasab was shelled and the shaikh fled, eventually to accept Muscati authority when the Bani Shatair Shihuh refused to support him.

### Sa'id b. Taimur and the Dissolution of the Imamate

Taimur was finally permitted to abdicate in 1931, and the sultanate passed to his son Sa'id, although he was not formally recognized until 1932. Sa'id b. Taimur had begun to play an active role in the administration in 1929 when he became president of the council of ministers. He was a well-educated (if not brilliant), ambitious, and conscientious ruler who was keenly aware of the humiliation that both his father and grandfather had suffered at the hands of the British, primarily as a result of the financial condition of the state. His main concerns were to maintain a

Barasti (palm frond houses) and fishing boats. Barastis are common along the Batinah coast because they offer low-cost housing well suited to Oman's hot climate. The small fishing boats made of palm fronds are used for fishing close to the shore; because of their open construction they float just below the surface, giving the appearance that their occupants are walking on water.

balanced budget, find new sources of income, and keep away from the British as much as possible. Accordingly, he spent a great amount of time in Salalah and pestered the British about the development of mineral and agricultural resources. When income from oil, in the form of exploration payments, began to come into Oman in the late 1930s, much of it went to shaikhs of interior tribes as Sa'id sought to enhance his reputation in the imam's territories. Sa'id could not, however, deliver access to potential oil fields in the interior to the oil company.

Oman drifted into obscurity. Al-Khalili remained imam until 1954, although bad health severely limited his effectiveness during the last decade of his life and only enhanced his proclivity to isolation. Isa b. Salih, who had for so long served to moderate interior politics, died in 1946 and was succeeded by his weak son Muhammad as tamimah of the Hirth. When Muhammad died several years later, a power struggle developed within the Hirth between Salih b. Isa, supported by his brother Ibrahim, and Muhammad's son Ahmad. Salih was victorious, but the Hirth were badly divided. Ahmad b. Muhammad began courting the friendship of Sa'id b. Taimur.

An unfortunate consequence of the Hirth power struggle was that Sulaiman b. Himyar al-Nabhani became the leading secular force in the imamate. Despite his public support for al-Khalili, Sulaiman b. Himyar was an ambitious, ruthless man who probably coveted the imamate but failing that would have settled for an independent kingdom of Jabal al-Akhdar. He began making overtures to the Saudis and harbored notions of cutting his own deal with an oil company. Al-Khalili also faced a raft of other problems. For most of his reign, Oman experienced a severe drought that nearly destroyed agriculture in the Sharqiyah and resulted in large-scale emigration to Zanzibar. Furthermore, the Saudis began to put pressure on the imamate's western frontier as ibn Sa'ud, encouraged by Aramco (the Arabian-American Oil Company), expanded his borders and occupied the Buraimi oasis in October 1952.

Al-Khalili died in May 1954, and the tribal leaders convened in Nizwa to elect his successor. Discussions among the imam and the tribal and religious leaders about a future imam had begun before al-Khalili's death. Several candidates were proposed, but some, like Sultan Sa'id, were not considered acceptable on religious grounds whereas others were too closely associated with tribal interests, especially any candidate supported by Sulaiman b. Himyar. The final choice was Ghalib b. Ali al-Hinai. Ghalib was a protégé of al-Khalili, who had overseen his education, and had served as qadi of Rustaq and Nizwa and as the imamate's treasurer. As a member of the Bani Hina, although not its tamimah, he was acceptable to the Hinawi tribes and their leader Salih b. Isa al-Hirthi. He was also favored by Sulaiman b. Himyar and his Saudi allies. However, Ghalib was not acceptable to Sa'id b. Taimur.

Because the political situation in the interior was in flux, Petroleum Development Oman (PDO), which held the oil concession for Oman, took drastic action. Desiring access to Jabal Fahud, PDO financed and organized the Muscat and Oman Field Forces (MOFF). In September 1954 MOFF accompanied a PDO surveying team to Fahud and then, despite an explicit order to the contrary from the sultan, seized the town of Ibri from the imamate. Sulaiman b. Himyar convinced Ghalib of the need to reassert control over Ibri and to establish a direct link with the Saudi garrison at Buraimi. The imam's army attacked Ibri. The sultan, seeing an opportunity to assert his control over the interior, now approved offensive action against Oman. The Batinah Force, formed in 1952, marched into the Ghadaf where it was able to defeat the imamate forces under Talib b. Ali, the imam's brother, and another Saudi sympathizer and capture Rustaq in late 1955. Meanwhile, the Trucial Oman Scouts expelled the Saudis from Buraimi in October 1955, thereby cutting off the imamate's source of military supplies and money. Then in December 1955 MOFF occupied Nizwa virtually without opposition.

The imamate dissolved quickly after that. Ghalib resigned as imam and retired to his home in Bilad Sait. Sulaiman b. Himyar retired to Tanuf, whereas Talib b. Ali and Salih b. Isa fled the country, both ultimately ending up in Saudi Arabia. Sultan Sa'id moved quickly to consolidate his position. Following an overland journey from Salalah to Nizwa in late December, Sa'id appointed Ahmad b. Muhammad al-Hirthi tamimah of the Hirth and made him governor of Nizwa with virtual sovereignty over the interior. The sultan then proceeded to Buraimi and Sohar before returning to Muscat. The Sultanate of Muscat and Oman was reunified.

# 5

# Challenges to Unity

Although Oman was officially unified in 1955 with the abdication of the imam and Sa'id's conquest of the interior, the country's difficulties persisted. The first challenge, in May 1957 when the supporters of the imamate staged an uprising in Oman to restore Imam Ghalib, was successfully quelled by Sa'id, with British support. No sooner had the restoration movement been suppressed than a second challenge arose in Dhofar where local grievances against Sa'id's tyranny were overlaid with Arab nationalist and Marxist influences, resulting in a revolt beginning in 1961. By mid-decade, it had become apparent to the British that the main problem in Oman was the sultan himself. A palace coup in July 1970 brought Sa'id's son, Qaboos, to power, and the young, modernizing, and popular new sultan completed the unification of the country by 1976.

## THE RESTORATION MOVEMENT

Sa'id was able to enjoy his newfound prestige as sultan of Muscat and Oman for only eighteen months. Talib b. Ali spent most of 1956 recruiting Omani laborers in Saudi Arabia for the Oman Revolutionary Movement (ORM) while planning with Ghalib, Sulaiman b. Himyar, and Sulaiman b. Isa al-Hirthi a simultaneous revolt throughout Oman to restore the imamate. Sulaiman b. Isa's premature uprising in May 1957, resulting from his dispute with Ahmad b. Muhammad al-Hirthi, was suppressed easily when Sulaiman was unable to obtain the support of the tribe. Sulaiman was imprisoned in Muscat. Imam Ghalib emerged from retirement at Bilad Sait later in the month and proclaimed the reestablishment of his government. He was immediately besieged by the sultan's Muscat and Oman Field Force (MOFF). Talib's ORM, armed with Saudi-supplied U.S. arms and mines, entered Oman via the Batinah in early June and proceeded, unopposed, to Bilad Sait; the siege was broken, and the sultan's forces withdrew to Firq. Meanwhile, Sulaiman

b. Himyar, who had been enticed to Muscat by Sa'id and placed under house arrest, was able to escape to Tanuf and raise the Bani Riyam. The sultan's troops were continually harassed by imamate ambushes, and they pulled back to Fahud. Ghalib's army easily occupied Nizwa and Bahla and seemed capable of driving Sa'id from the interior.

The sultan, virtually powerless, requested British help. After Parliamentary debate, the British government agreed to provide military assistance: A company of Cameroonians was sent to Oman, and air support from RAF (Royal Air Force) bases at Sharjah was promised. Overall direction of military operations was entrusted to General J.A.R. Robertson. Robertson's Cameroonians, accompanied by remnants of the sultan's army and Trucial Oman Scouts, left Ibri in August and easily occupied Firq, Nizwa, and Bahla. Sa'id's Muscat regiment had, meanwhile, marched up Wadi Sama'il and joined with Robertson's forces. The pacification of the Jawf was completed with few losses, although the picturesque forts at Nizwa and Bahla were damaged by RAF strafing.

Ghalib, Talib, and Sulaiman b. Himyar withdrew their supporters to Jabal al-Akhdar to continue resistance to the sultan. Their position was nearly impregnable because the difficult approaches to the mountain were easily defensible, caves in the mountains provided shelter for troops and supplies, and the surrounding villages provided friendly support, food and shelter, and transfer points for smuggled arms and supplies from Saudi Arabia. In addition to mining roads and ambushing military convoys in Wadi Sama'il and elsewhere, imamate forces began a propaganda campaign from Cairo and terrorist actions against Oman's few overseas interests.

With the withdrawal of the Cameroonians in August, Sultan Sa'id lacked the means to end the rebellion. In July 1958 he again sought British assistance, and in an exchange of letters the British government promised to help expand, train, and supply officers and equipment to the Sultan's Armed Forces (SAF) and finance and supervise development program for Oman. Colonel David Smiley was seconded from the British army and sent to Muscat to organize SAF and expel the imamate forces from Jabal al-Akhdar. Smiley faced a difficult task: First the routes to the mountain had to be secured to prevent smuggling and then the strongholds in the mountains attacked. SAF secured the former in fall 1958 and even found an unguarded track up the mountain from the Wadi Bani Kharus. In 1959 Smiley, requiring more help, requested and received a contingent of British Special Air Service (SAS) personnel to be used in the final assault. That came on the evening of January 27-28, 1959, and SAS met almost no opposition. Ghalib, Talib, and Sulaiman escaped down the mountain and made their way to Sharqiyah, where they were almost captured, and then on to Suwayq and by dhow to

Saudi Arabia. Some mining of roads continued through 1959 but the leaderless revolt soon dissolved.

Opposition to the sultanate continued from abroad as training camps were set up in Saudi Arabia and later Iraq, and the propaganda office remained active in Cairo. A negotiated settlement was attempted, but several meetings in 1960-1961 failed to bring any solution. Little occurred in Oman, save the mining of a few roads. However, the setting up of a gendarmerie to capture terrorists and more strenuous patrolling of the Batinah coast with the subsequent seizure of a dhow filled with mines and rebels led to the capture of many leaders in Oman and an end to the terrorism.

## THE DHOFAR WAR

Sultan Sa'id disliked the whole Oman affair and desired to be free of the problems of that part of his country. He totally abandoned Muscat for Salalah where he completely isolated himself from his people and the British and his only communication was an occasional threat to declare the independence of Dhofar and leave the Omanis to their own devices. Sa'id soon discovered, however, that his attitude of benign neglect and petty restrictions had alienated even the subjects of Dhofar, a situation exacerbated by a severe drought in the late 1950s that decimated Dhofari agriculture. Despite its prohibition, hundreds of Dhofaris emigrated to the oil fields and military forces of neighboring Gulf states where they met with other opponents of Sultan Sa'id and began to organize.

In 1962 Dhofari rebels who opposed Sa'id blew up an oil exploration vehicle and sniped at Omani military installations within Dhofar itself. Although various opposition groups were formed, some with Saudi backing, others pro-Nasserist, Sa'id's security forces successfully captured about forty insurgents in coastal villages and forced the remainder to flee to the mountains. To cut the remaining malcontents off from supplies, the sultan encircled Salalah with barbed wire and denied access to all outsiders. This action further alienated the Dhofari tribespeople who depended on the markets of Salalah to sell their produce and obtain the few necessities of life.

By June 1965 the revolt had entered a second, more formal phase. The opposition groups held their first congress in the mountains of Dhofar and formed the Dhofar Liberation Front (DLF), drew up a manifesto, divided Dhofar into operational zones, and began launching raids against the government. The movement was controlled by tribally oriented separatists, like Musallim b. Nufl of the Bait Kathir, who saw the rebellion as a continuation of previous attempts to break away from

Sultan's palace (right) and the Portuguese forts in Muscat. Old and new exist side by side in the capital city of Muscat. Forts Mirani and Jalali, built by the Portuguese in the sixteenth century, are still in use. Sultan Qaboos's new palace, built in the early 1970s, and various government offices now occupy much of the old walled portion of the city.

Al Bu Sa'id rule. Opposition activities were still limited, however, because the rebels had neither the material resources nor the popular support necessary for a general uprising. The highway between Salalah and Thamarit, the main link with the mountains and with Oman, was harassed and several police stations in coastal towns attacked. The conflict involved little of international note until April 1966 when members of the sultan's Dhofar force, by then thoroughly infiltrated by rebels, barely missed assassinating Sa'id. In response the sultan tightened security around Salalah even further, increased his own isolation, and brought the predominately Baluchi SAF to Dhofar.

Still lacking a notable success, the DLF was reorganized at its September 1968 congress at Hamrin. Radical leftist elements under Muhammad b. Ahmad al-Ghassani, a native of Salalah, gained control of the movement and sought to change it from a poorly organized tribal revolt against specific grievances into an international socialist, Arab nationalist, ideological struggle against imperialist forces throughout the Gulf region. The new name adopted for the organization, the Popular Front for the Liberation of the Occupied Arabian Gulf (PFLOAG), clearly demonstrated that orientation. PFLOAG gained material and moral support from the USSR, China, and Iraq and was supplied with a base and headquarters at Hauf just across the Omani border with South Yemen, which had become independent under a Marxist government in 1967. Popular support was more difficult to come by. PFLOAG commissars, appealing to Marxism to gain supporters, set up agricultural collectives and sent children to South Yemen for education and recruits to the Soviet Union for military and ideological training. They also preached against Islam. Those who opposed these actions found their cattle and lands confiscated and their children taken away; in extreme cases, they were even killed. The Jibalis soon found the neglect of Sa'id replaced by the tyranny of PFLOAG.

Although its attempts at gaining popular support largely failed, PFLOAG was able to become more aggressive militarily with its new arms. Hit and miss ambushes were replaced by more serious mortar attacks on the Salalah Plain. During 1968 the rebels took the offensive, gained control of the western coast of Dhofar, and captured Rakhyut in 1969. PFLOAG also controlled the mountains. By 1970 the rebels had caches of weapons and ammunition stored in caves, such as the Shershitti complex, and had succeeded in isolating Salalah, which was subjected to regular mortar attacks. The eastern part of the Salalah Plain was also under rebel control. At its peak the rebel forces included 2,000 full-time guerrillas and 4,000 part-time militia and civilian supporters.

The rebel successes, which resulted more from Sa'id's gross inability to handle the situation than from the effectiveness of the rebels, served to encourage opposition elsewhere within the sultanate. In June 1970 a disparate group of foreign-educated Omanis of varied ideological persuasions and some locals who simply hated the sultan formed their own liberation organization—the National Democratic Front for the Liberation of Oman and the Arab Gulf (NDFLOAG)—with Iraqi support. NDFLOAG, with fewer than a hundred followers, immediately initiated mortar attacks on Izki and Nizwa. These attacks failed, and most of the perpetrators were captured. Information gained from these prisoners enabled Sa'id's security forces to arrest nearly all the leaders in Matrah. Another group, the Arab Action party, led by Abdallah b. Thani al-Shihuhi, was formed in Masandam.

## THE COUP OF 1970 AND VICTORY IN DHOFAR

The outbreak of insurgency action in northern Oman and the growing success of PFLOAG in Dhofar served to galvanize pro-regime opposition to Sa'id b. Taimur. The focus of Sa'id's opponents inside

Oman, and that of Oman's British allies, was the sultan's son Qaboos. Qaboos was born in November 1940 to Sa'id's Qara wife in Salalah. His early years were spent in Salalah until he was sent to public school in England and then to the British military academy at Sandhurst. Before returning to Salalah he spent a tour of duty with the British army in West Germany, trained in municipal administration in England, and went on a world tour. Back in Salalah the crown prince was kept under house arrest, ostensibly studying Islamic law, and denied all visitors except a few well-screened Omanis and expatriates whose loyalty to Sa'id was unquestioned. With the government crumbling around them, though, even some of these people became alienated and began to conspire with Qaboos for a change.

By 1970 Qaboos was prepared to take action. The groundwork had been laid with his contacts in Salalah including Buraik b. Hamud al-Ghafiri, son of the governor of Dhofar, Hamad b. Hamud Al Bu Sa'id, Sa'id's personal secretary, and Tim Landen, a SAF intelligence officer and former classmate of Qaboos at Sandhurst. Qaboos' Muscat contacts included the managing director of PDO—one of the few expatriates who was allowed to visit Qaboos regularly—and the sultan's new defense secretary, Colonel Hugh Oldam. The British secured the support of Sayyid Tariq b. Taimur, Sa'id's uncle, who lived in exile in West Germany and who was the most influential member of the royal family and a possible challenger to Qaboos' position.

The failed NDFLOAG raids in June 1970 provided the immediate impetus for the coup. On July 23 Buraik b. Hamud led a group of Hawasina tribespeople past the bribed palace guards in Salalah and into Sa'id's apartment. The sultan was not totally unprepared: He and his personal bodyguard greeted Buraik and his party with gunfire. Buraik, wounded, was forced to retreat but, with the backing of some Baluchi SAF soldiers, made a second attempt. Sa'id, who had shot himself in the foot during the initial engagement, realized the futility of his position and surrendered. He was then taken to the RAF base at Salalah, returned to the palace because he had not signed the abdication note, and finally flown to Bahrain for medical treatment. Sa'id settled in exile in London where he died in 1972.

On July 26 Sultan Qaboos, addressing his nation for the first time on radio, announced the change in government and his plans for the future. Several days later he visited Muscat for the first time and began to plan for political and economic modernization. His first priority remained, however, the Dhofar war. Within the year, SAF began taking aggressive action against the rebels. Qaboos announced a pardon for all surrendering rebels, and those tribespeople who had been dissatisfied with PFLOAG but had had to support the rebels began to defect to the government. These were used as the basis for the firqat, a Dhofari militia. The military campaign was put under the civilian control of the Dhofar Development Committee under the wali of Dhofar, Buraik b. Hamud al-Ghafiri, which coordinated military, intelligence, and development activities. SAF was reorganized with the establishment of the Dhofar Brigade, a 10,000-person multinational force, including Omanis (mostly Baluchis) and British troops, including a contingent of SAS and RAF. Other foreigners, most notably the Imperial Iranian Battle Group and Jordanian engineers, also provided support.

PFLOAG responded to these reforms by trying to interject some new life into the movement. At a party conference held in June 1971, the PFLOAG proclaimed a new program; later in the year it absorbed the remainder of NDFLOAG and adopted another name—Popular Front for the Liberation of Oman and the Arab Gulf (PFLOAG). Although the offensive against SAF continued during the first year after the coup, by fall 1971 the political changes in Oman had begun to tell on PFLOAG. Divisions within the movement between the Marxist radicals and Dhofari nationalists began to erupt; the latter tried to seize control of the movement in September 1971 and, when they failed, began defecting to the government, especially after a PFLOAG purge of nationalists in November 1971.

Government military strategy focused on cutting rebel supply lines and securing positions in the Jabal. In 1971 with Operation Jaguar SAF began attacking the rebels and occupied the Jabal Samhan during spring and early summer before withdrawing with the coming of the monsoon. In the autumn, work on the Hammer Line began with a series of pickets set up along the mountains, about 25 miles (40 km) west of Salalah, designed to slow down rebel movements. Then in April 1972 the government gained an important psychological victory by occupying Sarfait near the South Yemeni border during Operation Simba. Sarfait was on high ground and did not command control of rebel supply lines, but the ability to hold the exposed and vulnerable position, which had to be supplied completely by air at great difficulty and cost, was a morale boost. The PFLOAG response was a coordinated offensive, including rocket attacks on Salalah airport and assaults on the towns of Mirbat and Taqa. The offensive failed and marked the highwater mark of the insurgency. Soon after, the hills above Salalah were cleared of rebels, and the town was not shelled again. To add to the rebel woes, Chinese aid ended in 1972. In a last effort PFLOAG made plans in December to spread revolt into northern Oman. This raid did not get as far as the 1970 uprising, though; Omani security forces uncovered the plot, arrested approximately eighty-five followers, and discovered several arms caches in Matrah.

PFLOAG continued to operate without opposition in the mountains, especially during the monsoon season when the area was shrouded in mist and when air support, so important to SAF, was impossible. SAF continued to focus on cutting rebel supplies with the construction of the Leopard Line in 1972 and its maintenance through the 1973 monsoon. The Hornbeam Line, actually an upgrading of the Leopard Line completed in 1974, effectively isolated PFLOAG forces in central and eastern Dhofar, where they were weakest, and set the stage for the final defeat of the insurgents as SAF's active defense turned to offense.

By late 1973 SAF was prepared to take the war to the Jabal. In the fall, rebels from the Samhan and Qara mountains were cleared. Critical to this process of pacification were civil action teams that were flown into secured areas and that drilled wells, set up a store, clinic, school, and mosque, and built a road and later an airstrip to improve communication. SAF was assisted in both military and civilian aspects of these operations by the paramilitary firqat. These irregular units were formed in 1971 with rebels who had surrendered to the government and were given weapons and training by the SAS. The first firqat unit, which had been multitribal, had failed because of quarreling among the soldiers. Thereafter, the units were organized along tribal lines and posted in tribal areas. Although difficult to control and largely ineffective as fighters, the firqat units were an important symbol of government trust and desire to assist the Dhofaris.

In May 1974 PFLOAG held yet another party conference. The meeting was marked by a rift between militant Dhofaris who wanted to continue the struggle and more moderate factions that advocated an end to the conflict and political opposition. The militants dominated, and under a new name—the Popular Front for the Liberation of Oman (PFLO), in recognition of the nearer horizons of the group—the war continued. Under whatever name, the revolt was in its last gasps: The insurgents faced insurmountable odds with a charismatic sultan, oil income, civil action team development projects, the firqat, the multi-national military force, and the lack of appeal to their cause. In September 1974 the government began what was to be the final offensive with the construction of the Damavend Line from Manston to Rakhyut. On January 5, 1975, Rakhyut fell. A last sweep from Sarfait cleared the west of rebels, and some time later the cave complex at Shershitti was captured. In October the rebel base at Hauf was attacked. Sporadic resistance continued, but not even the temporary introduction of South Yemeni regular army troops in late 1975 could save the rebellion. At the National Day celebration in November 1976, Qaboos confidently announced to his people and the world that Oman was completely reunited and at peace.

# 6

# Political Development

The development of political institutions is very much a twentieth-century phenomenon in Oman. Throughout Omani history the governments of both sultans and imams were limited to the ruler, one or two advisers, governors or walis in the major towns who were assisted by qadis, and tribal levies raised during times of military necessity. During the twentieth century this structure began to undergo fundamental change in Muscat as the British became increasingly concerned about the survival of the sultanate. A modern cabinet was introduced under Sultan Taimur b. Faisal in 1921 and continued to operate, with periodic modifications, under Sultan Sa'id b. Taimur. After the 1970 coup the government expanded significantly, and Omanis began to play an increasing role in administration, although the basic principles of the political system remained essentially unchanged.

## GOVERNMENT TO 1970

Modernization of the government of the Sultanate in the early twentieth century was a consequence of British fear that, if something was not done in Muscat, the Al Bu Sa'id regime would fall to the imamate. Fortunately, Britain had only to deal with Sultan Taimur, who greatly desired abdication and retirement to either India or Dhofar to life as sultan of Muscat and who was happy to leave the burden of government to others. Accordingly, a series of reforms was instituted.

### Initial Groundwork

Finance was the first concern. The sultanate's income came primarily from customs revenues and the zakat (religious tax) levied on agricultural produce and various subsidies and loans provided by the British. Expenses always exceeded income in large part because of the necessity of providing for the royal family, so that successive sultans were deeply in debt to Muscat's merchant community. Although the practice of farming the customs had ended in 1899 and those revenues increased, the situation had not improved. The British solution was to extend a loan to the sultan to cover all his debts. In exchange, to ensure the repayment of the loan and keep finances under control a British financial officer, known as the wazir, managed the treasury and prepared an annual budget. The customs house was also reorganized and Egyptian specialists put over it.

Other administrative affairs were to be handled by a four-person council of ministers established in 1920. This council, like all later governments in Oman, was dominated by the Al Bu Sa'id, minority residents, and British advisers. Sayyid Nadir b. Faisal, Taimur's brother, was president of the council with another Al Bu Sa'id family member as finance minister. Zubair b. Ali al-Hutti, a Baluch who had served as Taimur's personal secretary, was minister of justice, and an old family retainer was in charge of religious affairs. In 1925 the British financial adviser, Bertram Thomas, was brought formally into the cabinet. None of these individuals was especially qualified for their positions, including Thomas who was far more interested in exploring Oman and the Rub al-Khali than affairs of state, but they did rule Muscat in the long absences of Taimur.

Military reform was a third priority. When the sultan's Baluchi and Hadrami mercenaries and tribal levies had proved incapable of defending Muscat against the tribes of the interior in the late nineteenth century, the British had sent Indian troops. A plan to replace these with a modern Omani standing army was implemented in April 1921 when the Muscat Levy Corp was formed, composed of approximately 300 Baluchis and British officers. The Muscat Levy was understaffed and poorly supplied, and its functions were limited largely to guard duty around the capital, civil aid projects, like road building, and ceremonial duties, but it did serve as an effective deterrent to the imam. Tribal levies still guarded the coastal forts, which were the seats of the walis, and the sultan maintained his personal guard.

### One-Person Administration

When the pathetic Taimur was finally permitted to retire in 1931 and was formally succeeded by his son Sa'id in the following year, the government underwent few changes. Sa'id, who had begun to play an active role in the administration in 1929 when he had returned to Muscat from schooling in India and Iraq, did scrap the council of ministers and replace it with departments of finance, internal affairs, and justice—an act that demonstrated more the new sultan's desire to control affairs directly than a fundamental change in government.

Sa'id administered finances himself, as he had done since 1929 when he fired Bertram Thomas. Sa'id's financial management system, based on the principle that the government did not spend what it could not afford, ensured that the budget remained balanced until the mid-1950s. When oil income began flowing into the country in the late 1960s, the sultan hired an expatriate financial secretary, but the office never really functioned as Sa'id refused to provide the bureaucrat with any information.

### Interior Affairs

During the first twenty-five years of Sa'id's reign, interior affairs were restricted to governing the Batinah, Ru'us al-Jibal, and Dhofar—although in the last the sultan retained personal authority and treated it as a private estate—and to maintaining contacts with the government of the imam in Nizwa. Walis, usually members of the Al Bu Sa'id family, were appointed to the major towns and performed their traditional roles as mediators. They and their qadi assistants were usually corrupt and much less respected than those appointed by the imam in interior towns. Sa'id also corresponded regularly with the imam and maintained personal relations with the principal tribal leaders. Sa'id also directed this department until 1939 when Sayyid Ahmad b. Ibrahim, a descendant of Imam Azzan b. Qais, was named minister of the interior, a post he held until 1970.

The reunification of Oman in 1955 and the suppression of the restoration movement of the imamate in 1957–1959 brought some changes to the interior department. Following the initial integration of the interior, Shaikh Ahmad b. Muhammad al-Hirthi, who had supported the sultan's efforts in Oman, was made viceroy over Oman, but he was replaced when the civil war began in 1957 with Sayyid Tariq b. Taimur, Sa'id's brother. Once the imamate was completely suppressed, Ahmad b. Ibrahim reassumed control over interior affairs and served as liaison between the tribes and the sultan, as well as dispensed tribal subsidies, but supervision of the Batinah walis and sharia courts was entrusted to Ismail al-Rasasi, the Palestinian wali of Matrah.

Several other administrative changes were made. In 1938 a municipality of Muscat and Matrah was established to govern those towns and to deal with sanitation, especially malaria prevention, water supply, and electricity. The justice department, which had continued to be administered by Zubair b. Ali al-Hutti, had ceased to function by 1939 because there was so little justice to administer, since the sharia, British consular, and various communal courts were under separate jurisdiction. Zubair became a personal adviser to the sultan, and judicial matters were handled on an ad hoc basis. Also in 1939 Sa'id appointed his

New mosque. Part of the palace complex in Muscat, the architecture of the new official mosque exemplifies the South Asian influence on modern Oman. Traditional mosques in the sultanate have very low minarets.

uncle Sayyid Shihab b. Faisal foreign minister to oversee relations with the British and serve as the sultan's personal and ceremonial representative during his long absences in Salalah. Shihab performed these duties until 1945 when he was replaced by the first of several British expatriates. Then in 1960 when Sa'id abandoned Muscat permanently for Salalah, Shihab again entered the government as Sa'id's ceremonial representative and governor of the capital area, and an expatriate, F. Chauncey, was named Sa'id's personal adviser to keep a watch over Muscat and deal with the British.

### Expansion of the Military

Sa'id's growing interest in interior affairs in the 1950s resulted in an expansion of the military. In 1952 after the Saudis occupied Buraimi, a second military unit, the Batinah Force, was established in Sohar to supplement the Muscat levy (renamed the Muscat Infantry). A year later the Muscat and Oman Field Force (MOFF), organized and financed by the oil company, was formed and then used to establish and defend the oil company's position at Fahud as well as to assert the sultan's control over the interior. As in the past, the army had a British commander and officers, and, by order of the sultan, the ranks were 70 percent Baluchi and 30 percent Arab, with only Arabs from coastal tribes permitted to serve.

Despite these efforts, Sa'id's military was ineffective. Accordingly, in July 1958 in an exchange of letters between Sa'id and the British government, Oman was promised military assistance. A British seconded officer, Colonel David Smiley, was sent to Muscat in 1958 to assume command of the newly designated Sultan's Armed Forces (SAF). During Smiley's three years of service and that of his successors, the size and sophistication of SAF rapidly increased as the understaffed existing regiments—the Oman, the Batinah, and the Northern Frontier (the old MOFF)—were joined by a Gendarmerie, the Desert Regiment, the Southern Regiment, including remnants of the old Dhofar Force, and the Sultan of Oman's Air Force (SOAF). The military was organized under a newly appointed defense secretary, a retired British army officer named Pat Waterfield; Waterfield, who had been the commander of the sultan's ragtag army, was also in charge of foreign affairs and intelligence, which had an expatriate director. As before, staff and field officers were overwhelmingly British, with some Pakistanis but no Omanis, and the ranks remained predominately Baluchi.

Although on paper a government existed, it was a mere shadow of what was required as Sa'id refused to give up any real power. He continually isolated himself in Salalah, maintaining contact with Muscat only by radio phone and yet demanding and having final say in all decisions, no matter how trivial. His subjects lived in abject poverty and were governed by arbitrary rules, and there is every reason to believe that Sa'id wished it to stay that way. The sultan was an anachronism: He had long suffered a shortage of funds, distrusted yet remained dependent on the British, and despised his own people for their backwardness and disloyalty yet by his policies contributed greatly to both those conditions. In 1970 a major government shakeup occurred when Sa'id was replaced by his son Qaboos.

### ESTABLISHMENT OF THE NEW GOVERNMENT, 1970–1972

Immediately after the coup of 1970, Qaboos faced a myriad of problems—the Dhofar war, popular expectations of change, minimal government institutions—none of which he was especially prepared to deal with because of his own lack of experience, general ignorance of conditions in Oman, and few contacts in Muscat. What he was not lacking was expatriate advisers, mostly holdovers from the days of Sa'id. Government came to be controlled by an interim advisory council dominated by expatriates under the direction of the military secretary, Colonel Hugh Oldam, who had replaced Waterfield in January 1970. One of the interim council's first acts was to invite Sayyid Tariq b. Taimur, Qaboos' uncle, to return from exile and become prime minister in August 1970.

Tariq's return and enthusiastic handling of the prime ministership so soon after the coup resulted in an immediate political crisis. This was caused partly by personality differences and mistrust between the prime minister and sultan; Tariq was better known, more confident, and more dynamic than Qaboos, who had spent several years in virtual isolation in Salalah. Logistic problems also arose as the respective roles of prime minister and sultan were never clearly defined. It is not even certain that Qaboos had approved the appointment of Tariq in the first place. Finally, the two men had fundamental philosophical differences. Tariq has been portrayed in several Western studies as favoring a constitutional monarchy or even republican form of government. In contrast, Qaboos' outlook was very conservative: He saw himself as the inheritor of the Al-Sa'id tradition of absolute rule.

Tariq's distinctive philosophical approach was very apparent in the Omani administration during the first year after the coup. Whether or not one accepts Tariq's reputation as a liberal, the scope and personnel of his cabinet differed greatly from those of any preceding one. Existing ministries of interior and foreign affairs were joined by new ministries of education, health, justice, information, labor, social affairs, and economy. The Al Bu Sa'id royal family still controlled the largest block of

ministerial posts, but these men, including Faisal b. Ali Al-Sa'id and
Fahd b. Mahmud Al-Sa'id, had, like Tariq, opposed Sa'id's tyranny and
gone into exile. Other cabinet members included Saud al-Khalili, a
prominent tribal leader, and Asim al-Jamali, a trained medical doctor.
There were no expatriates: It was a cabinet of national reconciliation
with few ties to the old order.

Qaboos retained direct control of defense, finance, petroleum affairs,
Dhofar, and the Capital Area, just as his father had. Even though the
Omanis who held the top posts in these departments resigned, the new
appointees had very close ties to the old order; the new governor of
the capital area and representative of the sultan was Thuwaini b. Shihab
Al-Sa'id, son of the former holder of the office; the new governor of
Dhofar was Buraik b. Hamud al-Ghafiri, son of the former holder of
the office; the defense secretary was Hugh Oldam, Sa'id's defense
secretary. Even Qaboo's personal secretary, Hamad b. Hamud Al Bu
Sa'id, had been Sa'id's personal secretary. The remainder of Qaboos'
advisers were expatriates.

Even without the power struggle between Qaboos and Tariq, the
transition from Sa'id's government to the new order was difficult. The
new cabinet was beset with problems: There was no clear idea of either
general policies or authority, either collectively or for individual ministers,
personnel lacked expertise, and there were staff shortages and almost
no coordination. Tariq's relationship with Qaboos meant that the cabinet
received little information, a situation exacerbated by Tariq's absence
throughout much of the first year while he was settling his personal
affairs in Europe and seeking diplomatic recognition for the new government. Tariq did not even have a secretary to handle his correspondence
in his absence.

Resolution of the power struggle came in December 1971 when
Tariq resigned his post. Qaboos was quick to assert his control over
the administration. He assumed the prime ministership—adding that to
the defense and finance portfolios—and set up a council of ministers,
with himself as chair and Thuwaini b. Shihab as deputy.

## FORMAL GOVERNMENT

Oman has no constitution. Absolute power is vested in the sultan,
who combines supreme executive, legislative, judicial, and military
authority. The sultanate is hereditary in the Al-Sa'id branch of the Al
Bu Sa'id royal family, which has ruled the country since 1744. No formal
principle of succession exists, although in the twentieth century rule
has passed to the oldest, freeborn son.

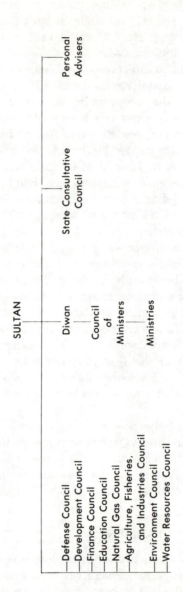

Figure 6.1  Formal Government Structure, 1986

SULTAN

Diwan

State Consultative Council

Personal Advisers

Council of Ministers

Ministries

—Defense Council
—Development Council
—Finance Council
—Education Council
—Natural Gas Council
—Agriculture, Fisheries, and Industries Council
—Environment Council
—Water Resources Council

### Administration

The main executive body in the land is the council of ministers (see Figure 6.1) chaired by a prime minister appointed by the sultan. The council includes the nineteen ministers who administer the specialized agencies of the government, the governors of the Capital Area, Dhofar, and Masandam, and various personal advisers to the sultan who hold ministerial status. The ministry of *diwan* (palace) affairs acts as the secretariat for the council of ministers, preparing the agenda and memorandum relating to meetings, facilitating communication between and among the various ministries and the sultan, publishing new laws in the official gazette, auditing state accounts, and administering the civil service. The principal functions of the council of ministers are to prepare draft legislation for proclamation by the sultan and to coordinate government policies and programs.

In addition to the council of ministers, the sultan is served by eight specialized national councils, each officially chaired by the sultan. These include the National Defense Council, set up in 1973 to coordinate activities of SAF, the Royal Oman Police (ROP), and the intelligence service, the Oman Research Bureau; the National Development Council, which is in charge of economic planning and all development projects above prescribed amounts; the Council for Financial Affairs, which draws up the annual budget and studies the financial allocations for economic development projects approved by the Development Council; and the councils responsible for education and training; natural gas; agriculture, fisheries, and industry; water resources; and conservation and pollution. Each of these councils includes personnel from appropriate ministries and representatives of the private sector.

Justice is administered by the Ministry of Justice, Islamic Affairs, and Awqaf. The sharia, specifically the Ibadi school, governs personal law and theoretically serves as the basis for sultanic decrees issued to deal with the wide range of matters not covered by religious law. The great majority of legal issues are handled at the local level in one of the fifty regional courts served by qadis. A three-member appellate court in Muscat handles appeals from the qadi courts. The sultan is the final appeal. Specialized commercial and traffic courts are located in Muscat.

Local government has changed little since the coup of 1970. The country is divided into forty-one *wilayats* (districts), two provinces, Dhofar and Masandam, and the Capital Area each administered by a wali who represents the central government and mediates in local disputes. Walis hold *majlises*, daily public meetings to ascertain local opinion and serve as an important conduit between the government and tribal leaders. All walis, except those in Dhofar, Masandam, and the capital area, report to the ministry of the interior. The three exceptions hold cabinet rank and are directly under the sultan. The municipality system, first set up under Sa'id, was expanded to other major towns in the early 1970s. These councils are appointed by the sultan, with the exception of Salalah which is elected. A brief experiment with elected rural councils was abolished by the sultan in early 1985.

### State Consultative Council

Perhaps the most dramatic change in Omani politics since 1970 was the creation in October 1981 of the State Consultative Council (SCC). The SCC is unique in the history of the Al Bu Sa'id regime because sultans have rarely if ever made any attempt to seek out popular opinion; the practice of holding the public majlis, so common elsewhere in the Gulf region, has never been followed by Al-Sa'id sultans. The SCC is a purely advisory body with no legislative power whose primary function is to provide a conduit for public opinion. The body originally had forty-five members but was expanded in 1983 to fifty-five. Nineteen of the members represent the government with ten of those being designated undersecretaries. The thirty-six remaining "popular" delegates are divided between eleven representatives of the business community and twenty-five regional representatives, although by sultanic decree all members of the council are expected to represent all Omanis. All SCC delegates are appointed by the sultan to two-year terms, which can be extended.

A seven-member executive bureau serves as secretariat for the council. The executive includes a president and vice-president, both appointed by the sultan, and two government and three popular representatives elected by the council at large. Four standing committees have been established, including those for legal affairs, economics, general services, and utilities.

The SCC meets four times a year. Its proceedings are secret, and— unique in Oman—delegates are guaranteed freedom of speech. Deliberations are restricted to economic and social affairs, and the council is charged specifically with making general recommendations in those areas and commenting on proposed legislation before it becomes law. SCC recommendations go directly to the sultan, who can reject them or pass them on to appropriate ministries for further action.

## POLITICAL DYNAMICS

Despite tremendous expansion in the range of government activities and greater participation by Omanis in their government's affairs, there has been little change in either the operation or principles of politics in Oman since 1970. As the formal structure demonstrates, the sultan retains absolute control over political affairs. Despite public statements to the contrary, Qaboos has shown little inclination to give up those powers. His own style of government differs little from that of his father as he remains very isolated from the general population and continues to rely on a small corps of personal advisers (in some cases holdovers from the 1960s) in those areas deemed most critical, such as finance and defense.

Qaboos has retained the prime ministership and the direction of finance, foreign affairs, and defense, and he continues to administer directly Dhofar, Masandam, and Muscat. Until very recently he has kept close watch on petroleum and commercial affairs through his cabinet appointees. These areas have come to be dominated by a group of Al Bu Sa'id family members, long-time business associates, and expatriates known locally as the Muscat Mafia. Prominent in the Muscat Mafia are Qaboos' earliest appointees, such as Thuwaini b. Shihab Al-Sa'id, Hamad b. Hamud Al Bu Sa'id, who became minister of diwan affairs, and more recently appointed officials. The latter group includes Fahr b. Taimur Al-Sa'id, the deputy prime minister for defense and security; Fahd b. Mahmud Al-Sa'id, deputy prime minister for legal affairs; Qais Abd al-Munim al-Zawawi, minister of state for foreign affairs in 1973 and currently deputy prime minister for financial affairs, and his brother Omar, a personal adviser, both of whom are the sons of one of ex-Sultan Sa'id's close business associates; Muhammad Zubair, minister of commerce in industry in 1974 and now a personal adviser, who is the son of Zubair b. Ali, Sultan Sa'id's one-time minister of justice; and Sa'id Ahmad al-Shanfari, the minister of petroleum and minerals since 1974, who is a member of the family that has most actively supported Al-Sa'id control of Dhofar. Added to this group is a number of British and U.S. expatriates in the defense and intelligence establishments who are in Oman either on contract or private initiative.

The cabinet has assumed a much more independent and active role in nondefense and finance areas as government becomes more complex and ministers become more sophisticated and confident. Qaboos, like his father, tends to isolate himself and ignore those functions of government in which he has little personal interest. The sultan deserves some of the credit for this turn of events as the council of ministers did provide some much needed coordination and a vehicle for discussion of policy matters. Also, younger, more capable ministers, like Salim and Ahmad al-Ghazali, the ministers of commerce and industry and housing, and Yusuf al-Alawi Abdallah, minister of state for foreign affairs, have made valuable contributions to the process.

Corniche in Matrah. For much of the twentieth century Matrah was the commercial center of Oman with the large merchants' houses and offices lining the waterfront. This prime real estate now contains apartments, banks, and a few shops. Matrah also was the recipient of early development projects including the construction of the coastal road, the Oman Flour Mills (background, right), and Mina Qaboos.

It is difficult to judge what the long-term significance of the SCC will be. Although ostensibly a representative body, the council is very much controlled by the sultan through his power of appointment, and it has been dominated by Al Bu Sa'id loyalists, the Muscat commercial community, and traditional elites from the interior. The newly appointed president, Salim b. Nasser Al Bu Saidi, is a member of the royal family. There appears to be little desire to turn the council into an elected body, and Qaboos seems very reluctant to introduce any form of democracy into the country, as demonstrated by the abrogation of the rural councils.

## DEFENSE AND SECURITY

At the time of the coup defense was Sultan Qaboos' primary interest, and it remains so today. The evolution of defense policy is also a good example of the process of change in Oman and the tensions between Qaboos' status quo orientation and the desire for institutional independence and nationalism. When Qaboos assumed power, the country faced a military crisis. Accordingly, the new sultan made few changes in the organization of the defense establishment, retaining Hugh Oldam in the defense secretary (a post he held until 1973) and depending on British and other expatriate officers. Defense spending was increased dramatically, though, as the military was expanded and supplied with modern equipment.

Qaboos is both defense minister and supreme commander of SAF. Operational command of the military is under a commander in chief, who also serves as principal defense adviser to the sultan. The SAF general staff has its headquarters at Raysut and administers the Sultan of Oman's Land Forces (SOLF), Sultan of Oman's Navy (SON), and the Sultan of Oman's Air Force (SOAF). Of the estimated 24,000 people currently serving, 20,000 are in SOLF with the remaining 4,000 divided equally between SON and SOAF. A 5,000-person paramilitary force, the firqat, serves in Dhofar with a similar force planned for Masandam. Internal security, customs, and coast guard and fire protection are provided by the 8,000-person ROP, commanded by the inspector general of police and customs under the ministry of the interior, and the Gendarmarie. Military service is voluntary, and because of the visibility and prestige of the institution it has no recruiting problems.

SAF has been well supplied with state-of-the-art military equipment since 1970. SOLF's two tank squadrons use U.S. M-60s and British Chieftains, whereas the armored-car squadrons are supplied with British Saladins and Scorpion light tanks. The artillery regiments utilize a variety of U.S., British, and Soviet (provided by Egypt) guns and mortars. U.S. TOW antitank and HAWK antiaircraft missiles provide defensive capability. SON operates Province-class missile boats and Brooke Marine attack craft, all armed with Exocet missiles, and landing craft. The royal yacht *al-Sa'id* also has military capability. SOAF combat aircraft include Jaguar, Hawker-Hunter, and Strikemaster fighter-bombers with an assortment of transport aircraft, primarily Skyvans and C-130s, and Augusta Bell helicopters. Air defense is provided by Rapier surface-to-air missiles and Blindfire radar. The air force has also ordered advanced Tornado fighter aircraft from Great Britain.

A priority within the defense and security establishment has been Omanization as the government has sought to replace British and other expatriate seconded and contract officers with locals. In the early years of Qaboos' reign the emphasis was on nationalizing SAF; the 70 to 30 Baluchi-Arab ratio was dropped and all new regiments were formed entirely from Arab recruits. Three of the eight battalions in SOLF remain entirely Baluchi. As Omanis gained military experience, they began to enter the officer corp. When Oldam left in 1973, his successor at the ministry of defense was Sayyid Fahr b. Taimur. At present an Omani, Major-General Hasan b. Ehsan b. Nasib, serves as undersecretary of defense and assistant to the chief of staff, and a second, Major-General Nasib b. Hamad al-Ruwahi, is commander of SOLF. Omanis also command all regiments within SOLF. The ROP has an Omani, Sa'id b. Rashid al-Kilbani, as inspector general. Despite these successes, Omanization remains an important issue: The chief of staff and the commanders of SOAF and SON are all British seconded officers, and some two hundred other seconded and contracted expatriates still serve in SAF. Qaboos refuses to put a time frame on complete Omanization of the military.

# 7

# Economic and Social Development

Oman's economic development began later and progressed slower than that of its oil exporting neighbors because of the country's minimal financial resources and its various political problems. The treasury was entirely dependent on customs revenues, the zakat (religious tax) collected on agricultural produce, and loans and subsidies from the British government. Although the discovery of oil and the beginning of exports in 1967 provided the necessary financial resources, the reluctance of Sultan Sa'id to spend on development and then the lack of financial planning after the coup of 1970 slowed the development process. By the mid-1970s, however, development began in earnest with oil and minerals providing the money for improvements in agriculture and fisheries and for the beginnings of industrialization and funding for wide-ranging social services.

## ECONOMIC AND SOCIAL DEVELOPMENT TO 1967

Government activities and services were always restricted by the limited funds available. Both Taimur and Sa'id had been interested in economic development, especially the discovery of mineral wealth to supplement Omani date, fruit, and fish exports, but early hopes, such as coal deposits near Sur and red oxide near Quriyat, proved illusory. Oil seepages near the coast at the northern end of the Gulf of Masira did, though, receive considerable attention. After Sultan Taimur b. Faisal granted assurances to the British in 1923 that he would seek their advice in awarding any oil concession, the search for petroleum began. In 1925 D'Arcy Exploration Ltd., a subsidiary of the Anglo-Persian Oil Company (APOC), received a two-year exclusive exploration concession and Taimur was paid R10,000 (R stands for rupees, which were used in Oman until the 1960s) in exchange. However, after a brief geological survey of the Batinah in 1926, D'Arcy allowed the concession to lapse in 1928.

During the 1930s interests in the prospects for oil in Oman were renewed. Sa'id wanted to award another concession but immediately came up against two problems: British insistence that he abide by his father's 1923 promise and the Red Line. In 1928 the companies forming the Iraq Petroleum Company (IPC), including APOC, Royal-Dutch Shell, Compaignie Francaise des Petroles (Total), Standard of New Jersey, Standard of New York, Gulf, and Participation and Investment Ltd. (Partex), agreed not to compete for concessions in Arabia, including Oman but to let IPC represent all their interests in the face of Aramco competition. The British backed IPC (a British company), and when Sa'id sought to assert his independence by sending samples of crude from Dhofar to Aramco, he was informed by the British that they had to approve all concessions. Although Sa'id repudiated the 1923 agreement, in June 1937 he awarded two concessions—one for Oman and another for Dhofar—to the IPC subsidiary Petroleum Concessions Ltd. (PCL). Sa'id received R300,000. Approval of the concession was delayed when the British and PCL concluded a general agreement that PCL would not transfer the concession to a third party without British approval, that it would employ British subjects to the greatest extent possible, and that it would grant to the British a right of exemption in time of national emergency by which the British government could take control of PCL facilities and provide oil on demand. The sultan was furious with these conditions because they raised doubts about his sovereignty, but he was given no choice but to accept.

Exploration was begun in 1938 by the PCL subsidiary Petroleum Development (Oman and Dhofar) Ltd. The geologists were most interested in the foothills of the Western Hajar but were prevented from exploring there because the area was within the territory of the imamate. A land survey of the northern Batinah and aerial surveys of Dhofar and the Huqf were disappointing, and PCL ruled out any hopes for oil. When exploration ceased during the war, Sa'id became increasingly dissatisfied, claiming that the company had no intention of developing the concession. He was greatly disappointed in 1944 when PCL picked up the concessions for both Dhofar and Oman. With British encouragement, a new survey of Dhofar was conducted in 1948, and when no oil was found, PCL gave up its concession there to devote its attentions to Oman.

After the war, interest in various economic development projects was renewed, motivated by the desire to improve the standard of living in Muscat and by the hope that prosperity might break down the isolation of the interior. As early as 1943 Sa'id had commissioned an agricultural survey of Dhofar. This was followed by fisheries and agricultural surveys of the Batinah in 1948 and 1950. Sa'id also granted a two-year exclusive prospecting license for Dhofar in hopes of developing mineral resources. Nothing came of these efforts. Muscat did, however, begin to see some of the benefits of the twentieth century. In 1948 Cable and Wireless Company was contracted to build and operate a telephone system, and in the same year the British Bank of the Middle East (BBME, then the Imperial Bank of Iran) opened the first bank in Muscat but only after it was promised a twenty-year monopoly.

A shortage of cash precluded any economic development during the 1950s, a situation exacerbated by the war in the interior, which put the Muscati budget in the red for the first time in twenty years. In 1958 Sa'id sold the exclave of Gwadur to Pakistan for £3 million. Also in that year he began receiving development aid from the British. The formation of a development department had been a quid pro quo for military aid, and although Sa'id did not like the idea, he accepted it. Sa'id's lack of enthusiasm aside, under Hugh Bousted and later D. Ogram the development department had a few notable successes, including setting up of health facilities, building roads to Sohar and up Wadi Sama'il, establishing agricultural centers in Sohar and Nizwa, and operating the two boys' schools in the Capital Area.

The reunification of Oman in 1959 was a boon to Petroleum Development Oman (PDO) as it eliminated the problem of access to areas of potential exploration. However, by 1960 four test wells costing $25 million had been drilled without finding any oil, and PDO management was unwilling to invest any more in exploration. A reorganization of the company followed with Royal-Dutch Shell taking an 85 percent interest, Total 10 percent, and Partex retaining its 5 percent. Exploration continued and oil was discovered at Fahud, only 400 yards (360 m) from one of PDO's earlier dry holes. Commercial production began in 1964, and with the construction of a $50 million pipeline and oil facility at Mina al-Fahl, exports began in 1967.

## BEGINNINGS OF CHANGE, 1967–1975

Oil exports and the subsequent rise in government income brought even more pressure for change. Sa'id began to bring in additional expatriate specialists, including a finance secretary and petroleum secretary. In 1968 a new development and planning board, also under expatriates, was formed, while the old development department continued to operate, and was given generous amounts of money. This new department immediately laid plans for Oman's future. A development scheme was drawn up for Muscat and Matrah, and new government office buildings were planned. Matrah was to get a new port. A new international airport was to be constructed. Schools, clinics, roads were to be built. Although progress was slow because Sa'id was against change, work progressed.

When Qaboos took control of the government, Oman had an incredible need for almost everything—roads, schools, health care, communications, financial services, water resources, housing—and high expectations that the new ruler would transform the country overnight. Even with the slight start that Sa'id had provided and steady (if not spectacular) oil revenues, that was not the case. First priority was given to suppressing of the revolt in Dhofar, and a lack of expertise and planning within the government hampered the development that was begun. Nevertheless, economic growth during those early years and during the past fifteen years has been spectacular as Oman, or at least parts of it, has been transformed from almost medieval conditions to a modern state.

An immediate problem facing the new government was a lack of planning and direction. This was partly the result of the power struggle between Qaboos and Tariq and of insufficient expertise among those concerned with development. The existing planning committee, dominated by expatriate holdovers from Sa'id's time, was understaffed and, although well intentioned, distrusted by the Omanis as some believed, incorrectly, that members were profiting from their positions. An Arab-dominated interim planning council was formed in 1972 to oversee the planning committee, but it failed. Its successor, the supreme council for economic planning and development, was also ineffective. Added to these institutional problems was a lack of procedures for development projects, with individual ministers simply approaching the sultan directly for approval of pet projects without reference to any development group, financial officers, or fellow ministers. Not surprisingly, during this period there was a tendency toward high visibility prestige projects.

Despite these difficulties, economic development in the early years of Qaboos' reign did begin to provide infrastructure and basic services. Sa'id's projects (Matrah port, Sib airport, Sohar road) were completed, along with a second port at Raysut, near Salalah, hundreds of miles of paved and graded roads, a communications network, with radio and television stations in Muscat and Salalah, telephones, an expanded postal system, and an earth-satellite station, and the first newspapers and magazines appeared. Social services such as schools and clinics opened throughout the country. Electrification began, and the search for new water resources, including the construction of a desalinization plant, was accelerated. Business growth, encouraged by the government's emphasis on private sector participation in development projects, was phenomenal: Banks, hotels, insurance, consultants, engineers, and a flood

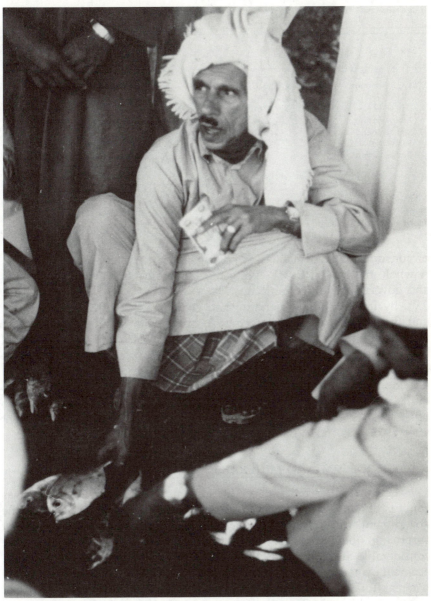

Fish auction in Sohar. Fishing, after farming, is the principal occupation along the Batinah coast. Fish, both fresh and dried, are a major source of protein in the Omani diet, in addition to providing cattle feed, fertilizer, and a valuable export. Since 1970 the government has actively encouraged the development of Omani fisheries both as a local food source and as part of economic diversification.

TABLE 7.1
Government Five-Year Plans, 1976-1990

| Plan | 1976-1980 (act)* | 1981-1985 (est)* | 1986-1990 (for)* |
|---|---|---|---|
| Total revenue | 3,357 | 6,947 | 8,044 |
| Oil | 2,860 | 6,376 | 6,374 |
| Non-oil | 266 | 343 | 1,200 |
| Loans/other | 231 | 228 | 470 |
| Total expenditure | 3,336 | 7,360 | 8,830 |
| Fixed | 2,348 | 5,138 | 6,477 |
| Development | 904 | 2,155 | 2,100 |
| Other | 84 | 77 | 253 |

*In millions of Omani rials (RO); $1=RO.345 (1976-1985); $1=RO.385 (1986)

Source:  Government of Oman

of consumer-related businesses sprang up to serve the import market. A whole new town, Ruwi, sprang up outside Matrah with new houses and government office buildings.

By late 1974 this spending had created a severe cash flow crisis, and the government was forced to borrow from commercial banks to meet current expenses. Help was also sought from the International Monetary Fund (IMF) whose financial and technical assistance laid the groundwork for the development law of 1975 and the formation of a development council. A primary objective of the new council was to draft a five-year plan, published in 1976 and since followed by two others (see Table 7.1). Freed of the drain of the Dhofar war, development after 1975 was much more orderly and rational.

## PETROLEUM AND MINERALS

Oil and other mineral production, most important of which was copper, dominates the economy, contributing over 95 percent of the government's revenues and financing other economic programs. It is not surprising, therefore, that this sector of the economy would receive considerable attention after 1975. PDO, which became 60 percent government owned in 1980 (Shell holds 34 percent and manages the company whereas Total holds 4 percent and Partex 2 percent), remains the principal producer, although Oman, unique in the Gulf region, has encouraged private concessionaires to explore for and develop new resources. Natural gas, traditionally flared at the wellhead, and a domestic refinery are recent developments, and copper production, begun in 1983, offers some hope of diversification.

TABLE 7.2
Oil Production and Prices, 1967–1985

| Year | Million Barrels | Price Per Barrel (Dec.) |
|------|-----------------|-------------------------|
| 1967 | 23.0 | $1.82 |
| 1968 | 87.7 | $1.82 |
| 1969 | 119.7 | $1.82 |
| 1970 | 121.3 | $1.82 |
| 1971 | 107.4 | $2.31 |
| 1972 | 103.0 | $2.62 |
| 1973 | 106.9 | $5.62 |
| 1974 | 106.0 | $12.30 |
| 1975 | 124.6 | $12.50 |
| 1976 | 133.8 | $12.55 |
| 1977 | 123.6 | $13.98 |
| 1978 | 114.9 | $13.07 |
| 1979 | 107.7 | $28.30 |
| 1980 | 103.2 | $36.61 |
| 1981 | 119.8 | $34.05 |
| 1982 | 118.8 | $34.03 |
| 1983 | 141.9 | $29.06 |
| 1984 | 152.8 | $27.66 |
| 1985 | 182.6 | $23.83 |

Source:  Government of Oman

In the early 1970s it appeared that Oman might be the first Gulf state to run out of oil: The country's peak production occurred in 1976 (see Table 7.2) and its reserves were estimated at only ten to twelve years' production. The main producing areas at Jabal Fahud and Yibal were providing steady production, but that oil was becoming increasingly expensive to produce. Accordingly, a twofold response was developed. First, PDO began applying secondary and enhanced recovery techniques, such as gas and water injection, that increased production costs but extended the lives of the wells. Second, the search for new oil was intensified. As the largest concession holder, PDO had the most early successes, bringing on line the Marmul and Amal fields in southern Oman, which had been discovered in the late 1950s but remained undeveloped because of their isolation and the heavy viscosity of the oil. Discovery of lighter oil nearby and the construction of a spur to the PDO trunk line eliminated those problems so that production could begin in 1980. PDO has since added the Rima field in 1982 and the Qarn Alam fields in central Oman in 1984 and 1986.

The Omani government also decided to grant concessions to foreign companies in territories given up by PDO. Two offshore tracts were awarded in 1973, one to Amoco and another in the Straits of Hormuz to Elf Aquitaine. Two years later Elf obtained the Butabul concession along the Saudi border. Oil was struck there and production begun in 1980, making Elf Oman's second largest producer. Other operators include British Petroleum in Dhofar, Occidental near Ibri, Japan Petroleum Exploration, Japan Petroleum Development, and Consolidated International Petroleum Corporation.

Exploration has paid off. Omani reserves are estimated in late 1985 at 4 billion barrels and production has risen from the low of 270,000 barrels per day (bpd) in 1980 to 500,000 bpd in 1985. Enhanced recovery techniques are still used, especially steam in the south with its heavier crudes, and experimentation with polymer injection is to begin. Plans are to increase production to 1 million bpd with a major limitation being the eighteen-year-old PDO pipeline, which now operates at capacity. The pipeline is being upgraded in stages. Omani oil goes to Japan and elsewhere in East Asia with secondary markets in Western Europe. The country is not a member of the Organization of Petroleum Exporting Countries (OPEC) but traditionally used OPEC markers to set its own prices. Oman is a member of the Organization of Arab Petroleum Exporting Countries (OAPEC).

The decline in oil production during the late 1970s did serve to increase interest in natural gas. In 1979 a natural gas liquids plant was built at Yibal, which added about 3,500 bpd in condensates to oil production. Dry gas was then sent via pipeline to Ghubra, near Muscat, for use in the desalinization plant and electric generators. A second plant at Yibal also recovers butane and propane. The former is used by the National Gas Company at Rusail to produce bottled gas for domestic use. Production in 1984 was about 150 million cubic feet (4.3 million cu m) a day with the bulk going to the Rusail industrial estate and the Oman Mining Company copper smelter near Sohar. The government is spending $25 million a year on gas exploration. There are no plans to export.

Completed in 1982, the 50,000 bpd capacity refinery at Mina al-Fahl meets all the sultanate's current domestic consumption. There are plans to double its capacity. A second refinery has occasionally been mentioned for Salalah. This 200,000 bpd project, to be financed by the Gulf Cooperation Council (GCC), was to be connected by pipeline to fields in the UAE or Saudi Arabia and was to serve as an alternative route to the Straits of Hormuz. The present oil glut—which forced the Saudis to reconsider several refineries of their own—and the upgrading of the Saudi pipeline to the Red Sea have led to a shelving of the project. No plans have been announced for the development of a petrochemicals industry in Oman.

Copper exports from the Oman Mining Company began in October 1983. The government founded the company in 1978 to develop the copper resources found at Lasail and Bayda near Sohar. Initial plans for the $213 million project called for the export of partially refined ore, but a $15 million electrolytic refinery was installed. Fifteen thousand tons of copper were exported in 1984, and reserves are estimated at some 50 million tons of 2 percent copper ore, giving the mines an estimated production life of twelve years. Some chromite has also been discovered.

## AGRICULTURE, FISHERIES, AND INDUSTRY

Traditional economic activities of farming and fishing continue to employ nearly 80 percent of the Omani population. After ignoring this sector during the first five years, the government has been directing ever increasing attention to it in hopes of developing food self-sufficiency, so as to cut back on expensive food imports, and possibly expanding it commercially for export. In line with general economic policy, the government's role in agriculture and fisheries has been to encourage private sector development while providing technical advice and support services through the ministry of agriculture and fisheries and financial aid through the Oman Bank for Agriculture and Fisheries.

### Fisheries Development

Oman's offshore fisheries, concentrated along the Batinah coast and south of Sur, provide approximately 60,000 tons of tuna, anchovies, sardines, abalone, snapper, cod, shark, lobster, and shrimp a year— enough to meet all local consumption needs and to provide small amounts for export, especially in varieties like lobster that are not suited to local tastes. Most fish are caught by the 8,000 or so fishermen living along the coast who utilize traditional dug-out craft (*houris*) equipped with outboard motors. Two private companies, the Oman National Fisheries, set up by the government in 1980 and transferred to the private sector, and the Oman Sea Company, operate deep-sea trawlers. Oman National Fisheries is also expanding into fish processing with the manufacture of fish cakes and sticks to replace imported items. A foreign concessionaire, the Korean Overseas Fishing Company, has operated since 1977 as part of an agreement running through 1986.

Government has actively encouraged fisheries development. The Marine Science and Fisheries Center in Muscat provides scientific data and is currently conducting, with U.S. assistance, a survey to determine more accurately the size and nature of Oman's fish resources. The Fisherman Encouragement Fund distributes loans for the purchase of boats and engines, whereas government-financed and -constructed jetties, cold storage units, marketing facilities, and marine workshops provide low-cost support to small fishermen.

### Government Support of Agriculture

Farming, like fishing, remains a small-scale operation with the country's 101,000 acres (49,000 ha) of farmland divided among 10,000 owners. Traditional crops, such as dates, limes, bananas, and coconuts provide sufficient produce for local consumption and even some surplus for export. Agriculture continues to be concentrated along the Batinah, around Salalah, and in interior oases.

By far the most serious problem facing Omani agriculture is the shortage of water. Greater use, resulting from diesel pumps, tube wells, and inefficient irrigation techniques, has depleted aquifers and resulted in some salt water intrusion along the coast. A Public Authority for Water Resources was established in 1979 to help rationalize water use, and the United States is currently financing a comprehensive study of water resources. More immediate attempts to deal with water problems include government assistance in repairing the traditional falaj systems, improvement in the spring flow in Dhofar, and construction of dams to capture and store rainwater runoff. An experimental project in Wadi al-Khoudh, financed by the United States, seeks to replenish Batinah aquifers. Similar projects are planned for Sohar and Quriyat. Another government survey of soils and groundwater resources shows promise of a 10 percent increase in farmland.

Government has also been active in providing other services to farmers. A nationwide network of agricultural extension centers and veterinary clinics provides advice and government-subsidized seed, fertilizer, pesticides, and vaccinations for animals. There are also several agricultural and livestock research stations and experimental farms. Transport, distribution, and marketing of agricultural produce are facilitated by the government-run Public Authority for the Marketing of Agricultural Produce.

Commercial agricultural projects have been directed toward the private sector. The government has taken the lead in establishing agribusiness schemes, such as the Oman Sun Farms in Sohar and Salalah, Oman Date Packing Company with plants in Nizwah and Rustaq, Oman Flour Mills in Matrah (which meet all local demand for flour and produce some cattle feed), and a banana processing plant in Salalah, and then turning them over to private corporations. Other agriculture-related industries in the country include the Oman National Dairy, Areej Vegetable Oils, which exports to the UAE, and the Oman Organic

Goat auction in Nizwa. Raising sheep and goats is the main activity of the country's small bedouin population. The men pictured here model traditional Omani costumes—robe, turban, and skullcap.

Fertilizer and Chemical Industry, which uses organic wastes as its feedstock.

### Industrial Development

Although accounting for only 2 percent of Oman's gross domestic product—$174 million in 1984—the non-oil industry sector of the economy has grown by 48 percent annually during the past decade. Government has avoided heavy industrial projects that produce basic materials while encouraging small- and medium-scale private sector development through financial and site services. This policy is well suited to Oman's needs with its poor resource base in terms of numbers and technological background of the population and of lack of raw materials, limited markets, but an experienced, free enterprise–oriented commercial class with sufficient capital for investment.

Industrial policy is outlined in the Industry Organization and Encouragement Law of 1978, which offered incentives to both foreign investors and local firms such as tax holidays, tariff rebates, protective tariffs, guaranteed government purchases of local products, and subsidized utilities. Finance is available through both the ministry of commerce and industry and the Oman Development Bank as well as commercial banks. Government construction of the 250-acre (100-ha), $60 million Rusail Industrial Estate near Sib, begun in 1981, was another encouragement. Rusail offers 160 factory sites served with roads, sewage and water facilities, cleaning and waste disposal service, and a central administrative complex with shops, cafeterias, and a mosque and a nearby housing estate for 5,000 workers. A similar industrial estate is to be built in Salalah, with smaller projects planned for Sohar, Nizwah, and Sur.

By 1985 some 3,200 industrial units were in operation in Oman, up from only 10 in 1970. Following the pattern of the rest of the Gulf region, the earliest industries were related to construction because the primary activities were building roads, housing, and government buildings. The first factories made asbestos pipe, cement blocks, tile, aluminum door and window frames, and water tanks. More recently industries have become involved in processing or assembling imported semifinished goods to replace more expensive imports. Omanis now purchase locally produced batteries, air conditioners, paint, light bulbs, spark plugs, plastic bags, flexible foam, and cookies.

To date the only direct government involvement in the nonmineral sector has been the Oman Cement Company's 624,000-ton plant at Rusail. This and the privately owned 210,000-ton cement plant at Rakhyut use locally mined gypsum and limestone to produce some 60 percent of the country's still substantial cement needs. Another major project under consideration, and one out of keeping with industrial policy to date, is an $87 million steel rolling mill for Rusail.

### Limitations on Development

Several problems face all farming, agriculture, and industrial efforts in Oman. First is the shortage of labor, both skilled and unskilled. In fisheries and agriculture Omanis have been reluctant to abandon private small-scale activities in favor of agribusiness. For example, Oman National Fisheries has had to hire Thai nationals to staff its trawlers, and much of the labor for Oman Sun Farms is provided by South Asian nationals. A second problem is competition from cheaper imports. Valuable farmland traditionally planted in wheat has been laying fallow because of Australian imports, and the cement industry has encountered considerable competition from the cement plants in the UAE, which have been dumping their excess production in Oman at prices that are competitive even with a 20 percent tariff. Finally, overproduction in some areas, most notably in cattle, has also caused difficulty. However, better planning and increased knowledge about local conditions promise to eliminate some of these problems.

## EDUCATION

One of the new government's first priorities following the coup of 1970 was the expansion of social services. In that year, only some 900 boys attended three schools, two in Muscat and one in Salalah, with thirty teachers. Illiteracy, disease, and poverty were a way of life for all Omanis.

Immediately following the coup, an aggressive campaign to expand educational facilities was launched. Emphasis was on numbers rather than quality; some schools met in modern buildings, others were held in the open air. Quality of instruction was also erratic as the country lacked qualified teachers. Nevertheless, success has been impressive. Education is not compulsory in Oman, but some 200,000 pupils, 90 percent of boys and 60 percent of girls, were enrolled in 560 schools in 1985. Emphasis has been on primary grades, and demand is so high that most schools operate split schedules, with boys attending in the morning and girls in the afternoon. Segregated classrooms are mandatory after the fifth grade.

Adult education has not been ignored. The ministry of education operates 160 literacy centers that served 13,000 people in 1984. The program also offers instruction in arithmetic and Islamic studies and child care, home economics, and sewing for women. Vocational schools, operated by the ministry of social affairs and labor, provide training in carpentry, agriculture, and business skills. Teacher training has also been a priority as the rapid expansion in education meant that the country had to rely on expatriate teachers, most of them Egyptian and Jordanian. Only about 10 percent of the 10,000 teachers are Omani nationals. Teacher training centers in Muscat, Rustaq, and Sur provide one-year programs for both primary and secondary levels. These centers also operate in-service courses for teachers and administrators.

A major advancement in Omani education was the opening in September 1986 of the $315 million Qaboos University at al-Koudh. Scheduled to be fully operational by 1990, the university will provide education for 3,000 students, both male and female, with faculties of education and Islamic studies, engineering, science, agriculture, and medicine. About 2,000 Omanis now attend universities abroad, with the majority going to Egypt, followed by the United States and Great Britain.

## HEALTH CARE SERVICES

Health care has had similar progress. At the time of the 1970 coup the country had one hospital with twelve beds, operated by U.S. missionaries, and nine government health centers. Oman can now boast fifteen hospitals and some eighty clinics and health centers providing over 2,500 beds. The pattern of development closely follows that of education with early emphasis on the construction of new facilities and treating existing diseases. In the late 1970s the sultanate received assistance from the World Health Organization and United Nations International Children's Emergency Fund (UNICEF), which recommended more emphasis on public health and prevention. Major health problems included trachoma, which affected 95 percent of the people in the early 1970s, malaria, and cholera, of which there was a major epidemic in 1971. The last has been eliminated, whereas the incidence of trachoma is down to only 5 percent. The government has established a training center to help in the effort to control malaria. The disease has been eradicated in Muscat and Salalah and along the Batinah but still remains a problem in the interior.

Government plans are to expand medical facilities by another 200 percent. Three hospitals are under construction, including the 565-bed, $226 million Royal Hospital at Ghubra and a 300-bed facility at Sohar, both scheduled to open in 1987. Staffing is a major problem because less than 10 percent of the 600 doctors in the country are Omani nationals. A nursing school was established in 1970, and the medical school at Qaboos University is scheduled to begin operations in 1990. Oman will remain dependent on expatriate health-care professionals (mostly from India and Pakistan) for many years to come.

## SOCIAL CHANGE

Like its Gulf neighbors, Oman has been transformed by oil wealth during the last fifteen years. Educational and health improvements have contributed markedly to the general welfare of the Omani people, and other services and increased employment opportunities have brought material gains that a generation ago would have been unimaginable. Although poverty still exists and services are inadequate, especially in more remoted regions of the country, the prospect for the future is bright. Despite changes, though, Omani society retains many of the features of its traditional organization and has not been immune to some of the problems associated with rapid economic development.

Family, both in terms of the immediate extended unit and the wider tribal affiliation, remains the focus of social life, influenced primarily by ethnic background and Islamic values. Grants of land and government loans through the Oman Housing Bank have facilitated the replacement of mud-brick houses with modern cement houses or even villas with indoor plumbing and electricity and such added conveniences as television and air conditioning.

Life inside the home has changed little. Marriages are still arranged, and marriages between first cousins are the preferred pattern. Dowries have been limited (although not abolished) by the government, which has also severely restricted marriages between Omanis and foreigners. Islamic laws permitting polygamy and easy divorce for men remain in force.

The home remains the women's world: Her activities are limited to raising children, tending to domestic affairs such as cooking, and visiting with other women. Few women are seen in public, especially in the Arab-dominated interior; those that do venture out are shrouded in black robes and usually veils. An exception to this pattern are Baluchi, Zanzibari, and Indian women, especially in the Capital Area, who can be seen without veils in public in their colorful costumes.

Life is changing for an increasing number of Omani women. The government has sought to provide far greater opportunities for the country's women than have some of its Gulf neighbors. Although they follow the Muslim regulations on segregation of the sexes in schools and medical facilities, women do mix with men occasionally in the workplace, and some hold administrative positions in government in which they supervise male employees. The women's branch of the Royal Oman Police, which performs various functions such as customs inspection at airports, is one of the most highly respected institutions in the country.

Despite these changes, men continue to dominate public life in Oman. But changes are occurring even in the male world. Economic development and an increasing role of government in society have created a wide range of employment opportunities, although employment patterns are somewhat bound by tradition. Although no formalized caste structure exists, certain categories of employment are associated with particular groups within society. Increasingly, the Arab majority is found in business, government, land owning, the army and police, and services sectors. The only manual labor deemed suitable by Arabs is taxi driving, perhaps a throwback to the bedouin tradition. Manual labor is performed by Baluchi or other minority groups or by expatriate South Asians. The reluctance of Omanis to perform manual labor has resulted in labor shortages.

Two major consequences of economic development are the growth of a middle class and increased migration to the Capital Area and Salalah. The latter has been the greater problem in the short term as those in search of better housing, jobs, and services have not always been satisfied, although Muscat and Salalah have thus far been able to avoid the slum suburbs common throughout the Third World. Government programs have been developed to slow this urban drift, but the lure of the cities remains strong. Oman's new middle class, educated largely in Britain and the United States, is just beginning to exert pressure for a greater role in the country's political, economic, and social development and can be expected to have a long-term impact on Oman.

# 8

## Oman and the World

Oman's isolation throughout much of the twentieth century serves only to obscure a long history of international contacts and diplomatic activity dating from at least the sixteenth century and, if one considers commercial relations, well before. During the nineteenth century in the reign of Sa'id b. Sultan (1806–1856) Oman reached the zenith of its diplomatic history when it concluded formal treaties with both Eastern and Western powers. With the collapse of the Omani empire following the death of Sayyid Sa'id, Oman's international affairs were intertwined in European conflicts, most notably that between France and Britain. By the conclusion of World War I, all its foreign affairs were in the hands of the British. Oman's isolation was punctuated only by an occasional incident of international importance, such as the Buraimi dispute or the Oman question brought before the United Nations, both during the 1950s. Not until the reign of Sultan Qaboos b. Sa'id did Oman again become a regular participant in world affairs and begin to assume importance in Gulf regional concerns.

### EARLY DIPLOMATIC HISTORY

Omani contacts with its Indian Ocean and Gulf neighbors are documented for several centuries. In the eighteenth century relations with Persia were regular if not always friendly, as evidenced by several invasions during the 1730s, but during the nineteenth century Al Bu Sa'id rulers of Muscat concluded marriage alliances with the Persian shah and other agreements that gave them control of Bandar Abbas and neighboring islands in the Straits of Hormuz. Oman also maintained relations with the Ottoman Empire, and Ahmad b. Sa'id assisted the Turks against a Persian invasion of Basra in 1775. For his efforts, Ahmad and his successors received lucrative customs concessions for their trade with Iraq. Indian states, too, were on friendly terms with Oman, and Tippu Sultan of Mysore established the first foreign embassy in Muscat in the 1780s.

The European powers increased activity in the Indian Ocean beginning with the arrival of the Portuguese in the sixteenth century and reaching a peak in the eighteenth and nineteenth centuries as conflicts in Europe spread to India. Thus Oman became involved with the West, first in competition for control of trade and then on a more cooperative basis with various treaties. Oman's first contacts with Europeans were hostile as the Portuguese sought and eventually succeeded in adding the Omani coast to their overseas empire. Muscat remained the center of Portuguese possessions in the Indian Ocean until 1650 when they were expelled. Thereafter, the Omani fleet was the scourge of the region as the Omani sailors, encouraged by the Ya'aribah imams, sought to replace the Portuguese as lords of the western Indian Ocean. The coming of the French and British, with their greater resources, reduced Omani maritime activities.

Oman's formal introduction into the world of European diplomacy came with the conclusion of treaties between the British East India Company, which was concerned by the activities of Tippu Sultan, the French (a letter from Napoleon to Sayyid Sultan had been intercepted by the British) and the Dutch, and Sayyid Sultan b. Ahmad in 1798 and 1800. Sayyid Sa'id b. Sultan actively pursued close relations with the British, participating in 1809 and again in 1819 in British naval expeditions against the pirates of the Gulf. In 1820 Sa'id even convinced the British to send land forces to assist him in the subjugation of the Bani Bu Ali tribe of the Ja'alan. Thereafter, relations were strained as the sayyid's continued attacks on Ras al-Khaimah and Bahrain disrupted the maritime peace that Britain had established with such difficulty, and Muscat remained the center of the Indian Ocean slave trade. In 1822 and 1839 Sa'id banned the sale of slaves to "Christian" countries (including British-ruled India) and gave the British navy permission to seize Arab vessels carrying slaves on the high seas, but he would not abolish slavery. Then in 1839 the British obtained the first of a long series of commercial treaties with Oman.

Although Britain was Sa'id's closest and most reliable ally, the sayyid also sought relations with other European powers. Contacts with France had been established late in the eighteenth century when the French colonies of Mauritius and Reunion provided a lucrative market for slaves. Later, Sa'id often found himself caught in the middle of Anglo-French rivalry in the Indian Ocean as he sought to balance his friendship with Britain against the commercial importance of France. A French consulate was opened briefly in 1808–1810, despite British protests, but relations slowed thereafter. Then in 1844 a formal treaty of friendship and commerce was concluded between the two governments.

Mina Qaboos. Originally planned during the reign of Sultan Sa'id, Mina Qaboos in Matrah was completed by the present ruler and is Oman's largest port, continuing a thousand-year-old tradition of maritime trade.

The third Western nation to become involved diplomatically with Oman was the United States. U.S. relations with Muscat had begun late in the eighteenth century when New England merchants, following on the heels of the China trade, became active in the western Indian Ocean. Although trade with Muscat was sporadic, in 1827 a Portsmouth merchant named Edmund Roberts discussed with Sayyid Sa'id the possibilities of a treaty that would regularize commerce between Oman and the United States. With Sa'id's blessing, Roberts returned to the United States, worked for the passage of a treaty of commerce and amity in Congress, and in 1833, as special agent, exchanged ratifications with Sa'id in Muscat.

In addition to receiving foreign embassies, Sayyid Sa'id was also active in sending representatives abroad. Oman was represented unofficially at the coronation of Queen Victoria in 1834, and in 1837 Sa'id sent an ambassador to London. Three years later an embassy aboard the ship *Sultanah* landed at New York and caused quite a stir because the ambassador, Ahmad b. Na'aman, and Omani crew were bedecked in their flowing robes and distinctive turbans. The *Sultanah* next sailed to London carrying a second mission to the court of Saint James.

After the rush of activities in the 1830s, Muscat became relatively isolated diplomatically, and few Westerners called at the port. Sayyid Sa'id, ensconced on his island paradise in Zanzibar, concluded several new and tougher antislavery treaties with the British as Britain became the only European power with any interest in Oman.

## ANGLO-FRENCH RIVALRY AND BRITISH HEGEMONY

The death of Sa'id b. Sultan in 1856 ushered in a new era in Omani diplomatic history as Western powers other than Britain again took an interest in the country. The first issue to be resolved was the dispute between Sa'id's heirs over his far-flung empire. Both Sayyid Majid b. Sa'id in Zanzibar and Thuwaini b. Sa'id in Muscat claimed to be Sa'id's sole legitimate heir. The rival half brothers agreed to British arbitration on the matter, and in 1861 Lord Canning decreed that henceforth Muscat and Zanzibar would be separate sultanates and that Zanzibar, the richer of the two, would pay MT$40,000 per year in compensation to Muscat. In 1862 the French, with renewed interest in Indian Ocean affairs, signed an agrement with the British by which the two powers agreed to respect the independence of the two new states.

With the Canning award and the Anglo-French declaration diplomatic activity in Oman accelerated, and Britain reopened its consulate in Muscat and concluded several new agreements covering the construction of telegraph lines through Omani territory. In 1873 an antislavery treaty was signed that prohibited the trafficking and sale of slaves in Muscati territory, although it did not abolish the slave trade outright. Also in 1877 the sultan agreed to a treaty of commerce with the Netherlands. The Americans, conducting an active trade in dates, opened a consulate in 1880. The French also became active in the port, and even Russian and German ships made occasional calls. Then in 1891 the Anglo-Omani commercial treaty was renewed with the addition of the Agreement Regarding the Cession of Territory by the Sultan of Oman, by which the sultan bound himself and his heirs "never to cede, sell, to mortgage or otherwise give for occupation, save to the British government, the dominions of Muskat and Oman or any of their dependencies." This nonalienation bond came to involve the British in a diplomatic dispute with France and served as the basis for virtually complete British domination of Omani foreign affairs.

A French goal in Oman was to establish a coaling station, similar to one the British had obtained in Muscat in 1854, to serve French ships in the Indian Ocean. Sultan Faisal agreed to lease Bandar Jissah, a small cove south of Muscat, to them in 1897. The British opposed the action, claiming that the lease violated the 1891 exclusive agreement. Faisal disagreed and was supported by the French consul in Muscat who stated that the exclusive agreement, about which he had apparently been ignorant, was a violation of the 1862 Anglo-French joint declaration. The British pressured Faisal by withholding the Zanzibar subsidy, prohibiting British merchants in Muscat from making loans to the sultan, and in February 1899 issuing an ultimatum to Faisal that he cancel the lease and fire a French sympathizer in his employ. Faisal attempted to hold out, but when he was ordered to board a British warship in Muscat harbor and threatened with the shelling of his palace, he acquiesced. The French were subsequently given access to a coal storage area in Muscat harbor, and the two powers agreed that the terms of the 1862 declaration excluded both parties from acquiring even a lease on Omani territory.

While the Bandar Jissah incident was reaching its climax, a second dispute arose between the British and French. As early as 1891 French consuls in Indian Ocean ports were issuing French flags to Arab dhow owners, especially those in Sur, thereby protecting them against search and possible seizure by British ships on the high seas for dealing in slaves. After the conclusion of the Bandar Jissah affair in February 1899, Sultan Faisal ordered the French to cease issuing flags to Omani subjects and wrote to the Arabs of Sur telling them to stop flying the flags. Little else occurred until 1903 when three Arab seamen holding French papers were arrested in Muscat. The French consul protested, claiming jurisdiction over the Omanis as French protected subjects liable only to the French legal system under terms of the 1844 commercial treaty. Subsequent Anglo-French negotiations resulted in a French promise not to issue any more flags and an agreement to submit the whole issue to arbitration. In August 1905 the Hague Tribunal hearing the case decided that the French could not issue flags to Omanis but that anyone who had been issued a flag before 1892 could continue to use it. The right was not transferable, and the possession of a French flag did not extend the benefit of French protection to that individual. It still took three years to work out the details of who had flags before 1892, but by June 1908 the question was resolved.

A third area of dispute—the arms trade—continued the Anglo-French diplomatic rivalry in Muscat. The distribution of modern weapons and ammunition in the Indian Ocean region had originally developed as an extension of the East African slave trade as rifles would be traded for slaves and those arms used to capture more slaves. There was also a secondary market for arms in the Gulf, Baluchistan, and Afghanistan. Zanzibar was the primary distribution point, with Muscat and Bushire serving the secondary markets. The abolition of the slave trade in Zanzibar did serve to diminish the arms trade in Africa, but greater demand for weapons in both Persia and Afghanistan in the 1870s and 1880s resulting from Russian and British pressures on their frontiers kept the market going. Britain became increasingly concerned about the trade because of its impact on the country's policies in northwest India and Afghanistan. In 1892 the Brussels convention on arms traffic banned all arms exports to territories below the twentieth parallel north. Zanzibar's supplies dried up. Muscat, lying comfortably north of the banned zone, regularly served by European steamers and protected by its various commercial treaties, became the center of the trade.

Although the British and the Italians, who were concerned about arms finding their way to the Somali coast, sought to eliminate or at least limit the trade, the French saw it as a way to improve their position in Oman and generally to cause difficulty for the British. A British effort to control the trade by requiring that all British subjects in Muscat register their arms traffic resulted only in having Indian merchants begin dealing through Arab agents or getting out of the business altogether. This change opened the door for an assortment of French-protected arms merchants to establish businesses in Muscat. The trade flourished. Britain then sought diplomatic means to end the trade. Although the commercial treaties precluded a ban on imports, the sultan was not prohibited from restricting exports. Privileges granted to British, Persian, and Italian navies to search Omani ships for arms did not help much as the trade was transferred even more to French interests and their ships were not subject to interdiction. A reconvening of the Brussels conference in 1907 accomplished nothing. Not until 1912 when relations between France and Britain had improved was the trade ended as Britain bullied Faisal into accepting a warehouse scheme whereby there was still complete freedom of import and export but no transfers of arms without appropriate government documents.

The entente between Britain and France and the outbreak of World War I had indirect impacts on Oman. The British, considering the declaration of a formal protectorate in Oman, tried to get the French to give up their treaty guarantees but to no avail. Then in 1913 the two powers reaffirmed the joint declaration of 1862. It was all academic. The last resident French consul in Muscat died in 1918, after eight years of virtual isolation, and in 1920 the last remnant of French interest in Muscat, the hard-won coal storage depot in Muscat harbor, was transferred to the British. This, coupled with the closing of the U.S. consulate in 1915, left Britain as the only foreign government represented in Muscat.

Between World War I and the coup of 1970 Britain clearly dominated Omani foreign affairs. A series of agreements, the first in 1901 when Sultan Faisal pledged himself to award any concession for the development of coal fields near Sur to a British company and a second in 1923 when Sultan Taimur bound himself to consult with the British before awarding an oil concession, ensured British domination of Omani economic development. A civil air agreement in 1934 gave the British exclusive control of aviation in Oman and ensured their access to a string of airfields constructed during the 1920s from Shinas to Mirbat.

The RAF was stationed at Masira and Salalah. Relations with foreign governments were handled by the British, and even the Omani foreign minister was a British subject. Oman was a protectorate in all but name.

## BORDER PROBLEMS AND THE OMAN QUESTION

Oman's major diplomatic problems during the 1950s concerned borders, which began to take on a new significance with the discovery of oil in the Arabian Peninsula. Borders had first emerged as an issue in 1901 when Britain feared that France might establish a foothold in the Gulf by securing an agreement with an independent shaikh who had managed to slip through their treaty network. The British were also looking for a naval base of their own. Therefore, they wanted to know what Oman's borders were so they would know what territories were covered by the Exclusive Agreement of 1891 and the Anglo-French Declaration of 1862.

Initial concerns involved the northern borders of the trucial shaikh-doms. Omani territory on the Batinah extended to Murair with a disputed gap along the Shimiliyah coast as far as Dibba. That small port was partitioned between Dibba al-Hisn, a southern village inhabited by Qawasim loyal to the shaikh of Sharjah, and the northern town of Bayah with its Shihuh population recognizing the authority of the sultan. Borders inland from both Murair and Bayah were undefined: Ras al-Khaima challenged Omani control over the Wadi al-Qaur and Dubai, and Ajman claimed authority in Wadi Hatta, whereas Qawasim and Shihuh fought over Wadi Mahda. The shaikhs of Dibbah, Fujairah, Khor Fakkan, and Kalba regularly confused matters by claiming independence and alliances with Muscat, which used this as a pretext for asserting historical claims to the whole Shimiliyah. British officials regularly denied those claims. Shihuh territory above Dibbah was considered part of Oman by virtue of an 1890 agreement between that tribe and Sultan Faisal, although the shaikh of Bukha tried to play the Omanis off against Ras al-Khaimah, resulting in rival claims of authority to his territory.

The most complicated challenges, however, arose in Buraimi, and these eventually involved Oman in an international dispute. The Buraimi Oasis region is divided among nine villages with five different tribes. Its control of access to the coast, via Wadi al-Jizzi, the Dhahirah and interior Oman, and the Trucial Coast, gives it great strategic importance and has meant that it has been much fought over. The Saudis occupied it throughout much of the early nineteenth century with the shaikh of Abu Dhabi exerting considerable influence when the Saudis were gone. The shaikh of Ras al-Khaimah and the sultans of Muscat also were

Central business district (CBD) in Ruwi. Since 1970 the new town of Ruwi has become the commercial hub of Oman. The new CBD now houses the sultanate's leading banks and commercial houses. The distinctive new ministry of communications building can be seen in the background.

involved in the region, but for the most part the tribes were independent of external control.

An actual border among the involved parties did not become an issue until 1933 when Saudi Arabia awarded an oil concession to Aramco. Naturally, the company wanted to know how far east and south its concession extended. Britain, representing Omani and shaikhdom interests—although without the knowledge of any of the leaders subject to the conflict—claimed that the border had been defined in two agreements with the Ottoman Empire. The Blue Line, contained in the unratified Anglo-Ottoman Convention of 1913, set the southern boundary, whereas the Violet Line in the 1914 Anglo-Turkish Convention established the eastern boundary. Sultan Sa'id b. Taimur was notified of border negotiations in 1936 and approved a border proposed by the British in 1937, but World War II ended talks before an agreement could be reached.

Following the war, the question of borders again arose. In 1949 the Saudi government laid claim to Buraimi and announced that the borders with Oman would be negotiated with the government of the imam rather than with Sultan Sa'id and the British. Although the British sought evidence for Sa'id's claim and the tribes of Buraimi proclaimed their independence or allegiance to the Saudis or Abu Dhabi, the Saudis forced the issue by occupying the oasis in August 1952. Sultan Sa'id immediately joined forces with the imam and gathered an army at Sohar to march on the Saudi garrison at Buraimi. The British prevented his taking any action.

In October the British and Saudis accepted a standstill agreement that allowed the Saudis to continue their occupation of Buraimi while talks progressed. By 1954 the two sides had agreed to arbitration, but almost immediately upon meeting in Geneva in September 1955 the talks collapsed. The British then expelled the Saudi garrison with Trucial Oman Scouts. In 1960 a UN fact-finding committee under Herbert de Ribbing, a Swedish diplomat, attempted to resolve the matter but accomplished nothing. Talks in 1963 were also unsuccessful, and the border remained divided between Abu Dhabi and Oman.

Just as the Buraimi dispute was reaching its denouement, Britain faced with another diplomatic matter concerning Oman—the UN investigation of the Oman question. In August 1957 a motion was put before the Security Council to consider the "armed aggression by the United Kingdom against the independence, sovereignty and territorial integrity of the Imamate of Oman." The motion failed to win a place on the agenda, but in September ten Arab states requested that the Oman question be put on the agenda of the General Assembly because the imamate had been invaded by British-led forces in December 1955. The issue was assigned to the Special Political Committee. In hearings that followed, the Omani representative stated that Oman was an independent state whose independence had been confirmed in the Treaty of Sib of 1920. The British, representing the sultan, responded that the sultan's authority over Oman had been recognized in international treaties, that the Treaty of Sib had not ended that sovereignty, and that military assistance had been rendered at the request of the sultan. Furthermore, the British concluded, the whole discussion was an interference into the internal affairs of the sultanate and was against the charter of the UN.

It is difficult to judge the impact that the UN examination of Britain's involvement in Oman had on the British, but in an exchange of letters in July 1958, the British formalized their military position in Oman and forced Sa'id to begin a development program. An agreement later in the year terminated the non-alienation bond of 1891. Once these agreements had been concluded, Oman again became a diplomatic issue. With British suppression of the Green Mountain revolt, the Oman question was again raised at the UN. Herbert de Ribbing was appointed chair of an investigating committee that submitted a report in August 1963. Then in December the General Assembly established an ad hoc committee on Oman that gathered still more information and issued a report in 1964 calling the Oman question a serious international problem and encouraging a negotiated settlement that would not prejudice the position of either side. The General Assembly followed with a resolution in December 1965 calling on Great Britain to withdraw its military forces from Oman and to remove all forms of British domination in the area and for self-determination in Oman. By then, however, the whole question had become moot as Sultan Sa'id was firmly in control of Oman, and the UN soon found itself concerned with more pressing matters in the Congo, Cyprus, the Middle East, and Southeast Asia. Oman ceased to be a concern for the organization and disappeared from world affairs; the only significant change in its relations with Britain was termination of extraterritoriality in 1967.

## FOREIGN AFFAIRS SINCE 1970

Once Qaboos assumed power in 1970, Oman immediately sought to end the isolation imposed by his father. Delegations were sent to neighboring Arab states, and the sultan's uncle Tariq b. Taimur divided his time between the prime ministership and diplomatic missions to Europe in search of recognition for the new regime. Those efforts paid off: Oman was admitted to both the Arab League and UN in 1971. Oman has continued to play an active role in regional and world affairs because Sultan Qaboos' independent foreign policy has occasionally proved to be controversial in the Arab world.

### Arab Gulf Neighbors

Qaboos' first foreign policy priority after the coup was the improvement of relations with his moderate Arab neighbors. Oman had outstanding border disagreements with both Saudi Arabia and the then Trucial States (which became the United Arab Emirates in 1971), the Saudis were supporting the imamate, and both states were potential sources of financial aid for development projects and the war in Dhofar. Qaboos traveled to Riyad in 1971 and met with King Faisal. Oman soon began receiving aid from the Saudis, as well as from Kuwait and the UAE, although Qaboos' use of Iranian troops and close ties to the British often strained relations. However, sufficient agreement existed among the Saudis, Abu Dhabi, and Oman for a settlement of the Buraimi dispute in 1974; the kingdom withdrew its claim and Abu Dhabi and Oman divided the nine villages between them.

Throughout the 1970s Oman cooperated with its neighbors in several areas. Regional operations such as Gulf Air (the national airline of Bahrain, the UAE, Qatar, and Oman), the Gulf News Agency, Arab

Gulf Labor Organization, and the Gulf Organization for Industrial Consulting were established, Oman joined OAPEC, although not OPEC, and meetings were held at the ministerial level on issues of common concern such as education, labor, oil, communication, and social welfare. In 1976 Sultan Qaboos invited the foreign ministers of the eight Gulf states to Muscat to discuss regional security. No agreements came out of the talks, but the meeting did prompt calls for the establishment of a Gulf Union. The outbreak of the Iran-Iraq war in September 1980 and the fear of its spreading to the rest of the Gulf, however, galvanized opinion among the remaining Gulf states of the need for greater military cooperation. Accordingly, at a meeting of foreign ministers of Oman, Saudi Arabia, Kuwait, Qatar, Bahrain, and the UAE in Riyad in February 1981 a Gulf Cooperation Council (GCC) was proposed. The heads of state of those states met in Abu Dhabi in May of that year and formally proclaimed the creation of the GCC.

From its inception, security has been the focus of GCC efforts. Faced with a hostile Iran across the Gulf, Soviet influence in the Yemens, alienated from Egypt because of its peace with Israel, under attack from radical Arab states because of their conservative political systems, and distrustful of U.S. policy in the region because of its continued support of Israel, the six monarchies felt increasingly insecure. Despite these overriding concerns, the GCC states have found it difficult to reach a consensus on defense policy. Although there have been several agreements—the $2 billion aid package for Oman and Bahrain to strengthen their defenses, the establishment of a joint command for a rapid deployment force of two brigades to be stationed in Saudi Arabia, and joint military exercises annually since 1983—no comprehensive defense agreement has been adopted.

Oman has led opposition to a GCC defense pact. Qaboos opposes both an integrated military structure and formal alliance in favor of strong independent defense forces with close cooperation in training and exercises. Two specific concerns are that an alliance might be perceived by Iran as an Arab military pact against the Islamic Republic and the conditions by which the GCC's rapid deployment force will be permitted to intervene in any member state. Sultan Qaboos has also been at odds with his neighbors on the role that the United States should play in defense policy. Oman favors close cooperation, as demonstrated by its access agreement and joint military exercises, whereas other members wish to distance the organization from both of the great powers.

Economic integration has been a second priority as GCC member states seek to eliminate duplication in industrial development and integrate economic policies. Although cooperation in defense issues has proven elusive, at least a basic outline for coordinated economic policy was reached in June 1981 with the Unified Economic Agreement, which included provisions for common labor, property ownership, and tariff policies and rationalization of capital-intensive development projects through joint ventures. This agreement was followed in 1983 by the Unified Economic Strategy, which set a goal of having manufacturing contribute 25 percent of gross domestic production for each state by the year 2000. Among the major joint venture projects under discussion are an electricity grid, natural gas, a GCC highway and railroad, a pipeline linking Gulf oil fields with the Gulf of Oman, and an export refinery in Oman.

Despite these general strategies, economic integration has proved difficult in practice. As in defense, Oman has favored a more nationalistic policy, fearing that its younger, less sophisticated and developed economy will be overwhelmed by those of Saudi Arabia and the UAE. Therefore, the sultanate has adopted protective tariffs (permitted under the unified agreement) for fledgling Omani industries and implemented legislation that limits the commercial activities of GCC nationals. At issue for the Omanis is the great diversity in government subsidies for industries and operational costs. Also, Oman wishes to see a greater share of GCC development investment in the sultanate, a desire that appears doomed in light of the decision to cancel the export refinery at Salalah because of the oil glut and more secure Gulf shipping.

### Regional Affairs

Qaboos' independent approach to Middle Eastern affairs has caused friction with his Gulf neighbors. Qaboos' friendly relations with the shah of Iran throughout the 1970s and his acceptance of Iranian troops to help in the suppression of the insurgency in Dhofar brought public condemnation from Iraq, Libya, and other radical Arab states as well as more muted criticism from Saudi Arabia. Sufficient pressure was forthcoming that Qaboos eventually obtained assistance from Jordan to assuage the Saudis. Early relations with the Islamic Republic after the overthrow of the shah were understandably very poor; Qaboos went so far as to offer assistance to Iraq. However, growing concern for the stability of the Straits of Hormuz, which Oman shares with Iran, and Oman's own vulnerability to attack from Iran, as evinced by the defection of an Iranian helicopter pilot who managed to reach the Omani oil fields unchallenged, soon led to a less bellicose attitude, and Oman has sought to mediate in the Iran-Iraq war. Oman's small Shi'ite population, the overwhelming majority of which originated in India rather then Iran, was not an issue, although there were public demonstrations, unheard of in Oman, and calls for financial support for the government of Ayatollah Khomeini.

Oman has also differed with its Arab neighbors in its attitude toward Israel. Qaboos does not perceive Israel as a threat to Oman and has publicly supported a solution that includes recognition of Israel as long as the political aspirations of the Palestinians are realized and East Jerusalem is returned to Arab rule. Accordingly, while Oman continues to participate in the economic boycott of Israel, Qaboos backed Anwar Sadat's peace with Israel and King Hussein's 1985 effort to obtain international support for joint Jordanian-Palestinian negotiations with Israel. Friendship with both Jordan and Egypt remains very strong.

Relations with South Yemen—for over a decade a principal concern of the Omani government—have assumed much reduced importance. For the first decade after independence, any hope of accommodation between the sultanate and the only Marxist state in the Middle East was precluded by Aden's unflagging support for the rebels in Dhofar. Even after hostilities had ended in 1976, South Yemen continued to offer propaganda support to the Dhofari rebels and to call for the overthrow of the Omani government, and Oman was concerned about the stationing of Soviet-bloc troops and Soviet bases in South Yemen. However, by the early 1980s the situation had begun to change as the more moderate regime of Ali Nasser Muhammad assumed control in Aden. The South Yemeni need for Arab financial aid and a Soviet desire for closer relations with conservative Arab states have been coupled with a GCC sponsored effort, led by Kuwait and the UAE, to bring about a rapprochement between Oman and South Yemen in October 1982.

The 1982 agreement on the normalization of relations included provisions for discussions on outstanding border issues, a pledge not to use foreign troops in aggressive actions against each other, an end to hostile propaganda, and an exchange of ambassadors. Several meetings on borders have been held, and ambassadors were exchanged in late 1985. The February 1986 coup in Aden that overthrew President Muhammad raised questions about the future of the agreement, but new President Haidar Abu Bakr al-Attas was quick to send a representative to Muscat pledging Aden's desire to continue the peace process. Improved relations between Oman and the Soviet Union would also seem to preclude future attempts by whichever faction eventually emerges in Aden to spread revolution to Oman.

### West and East

Another cause for friction between Qaboos and his Arab neighbors has been his close relations with the West. Following a long-established historical pattern, Great Britain remains Oman's closest ally and exerts tremendous influence within the sultanate. With 11,000 British expatriates serving as consultants, technicians, and supervisory personnel, British firms have certain advantages in obtaining government development contracts. The British government facilitates matters by providing financial support through the British Export Credits Guarantee Department. The greatest influence continues to be in the defense establishment, in which British seconded officers still serve as chief of staff and commanders of both the air force and navy, and several hundred others serve in all branches of the military and in intelligence. In addition, the British corporation AirServices, is the major consultant to the Omani ministry of defense. In 1985 this close relationship was strengthened with the concluding of a $350 million contract between British Aerospace and the Omani military for the purchase of Tornado fighter planes.

U.S. relations with Oman were resumed during World War II when U.S. Army Air Force personnel were active in upgrading air facilities at Ras al-Hadd and Masira; these then ended in 1946 and began anew after the coup. Close relations were established in the 1970s as Qaboos supported U.S. initiatives for peace in the Middle East and shared U.S. concerns over the growth of the Soviet presence in the Indian Ocean region. Britain's withdrawal from the Gulf, the Iranian revolution, Soviet invasion of Afghanistan, Iran-Iraq war, and growing concern for the security of the Straits of Hormuz—especially with President Jimmy Carter's announcement proclaiming the Gulf as vital to U.S. interests—brought the relationship even closer.

The desire for a formal Omani-U.S. military relationship began as early as 1977 when the United States first sought access to the Masirah air base then being abandoned by the RAF. No agreement was reached until 1980 when the U.S. military was granted limited access to air bases at Sib, Masira, and Thamarit and naval bases at Muscat and Salalah. The nature of the access was cause for much debate. Both sides have been careful to distinguish between bases—where there would be a permanent presence—and facilities. According to Qaboos, the United States will be granted access to Omani bases only at the request of the Omani government or a majority of GCC states and only in the case of a direct threat that they cannot repulse with their own forces. The United States has stockpiled supplies for use by the Central Command, formerly known as the Rapid Deployment Force, and has carried on joint exercises with SAF since 1981. However, each U.S. aircraft must request landing rights.

The access agreement included a commitment for military and economic assistance. As a result a $320 million program is being administered by the U.S. Army Corps of Engineers to upgrade the

Chamber of Commerce building, Ruwi. With the long Omani tradition of commercial activity and the government's commitment to private sector development, the future for the business class, now led by the Chamber of Commerce, appears bright. The new Chamber of Commerce building is situated in the central business district.

facilities to which the United States has access. Economic aid has been restricted because Oman's high gross national product approaches legal limits established by the U.S. Congress, but the U.S.-Oman Joint Commission is administering programs on water resources and education. This aid has brought about much greater participation by U.S. companies in development projects, most notably in the strategically important Masandam region. Relations have also been strengthened by Sultan Qaboos' support of cultural programs in the United States, most notably the endowing of a chair on the national symphony in Washington, D.C., and the library of the Middle East Center, also in Washington.

Throughout the 1970s relations with the Soviet bloc were precluded by Communist support for South Yemen and the insurgents in Dhofar. The People's Republic of China was the first Communist state to end its aid to the rebels and seek a normalization of relations with Oman. Those efforts were successful; in 1978 relations were established and an embassy opened in Muscat the following year. There has since been increasing cooperation in economic and cultural areas, most notably the 1980 Sinbad Project in which an Omani native craft sailed from Muscat to Canton in a recreation of a medieval trading mission.

The decade also saw strong Omani distrust for the Soviet Union. Qaboos, given Soviet support of South Yemen, perceived the Soviets as the greatest direct threat to his government and to those of his conservative neighbors. The end of the war in Dhofar, rapprochement with South Yemen, and Soviet desires for improved relations with conservative Arab states did lead to discussions between the two governments, which resulted in the September 1985 establishment of diplomatic relations. Omani motivations for the move, which came as a surprise to most Western observers, are complex. Public explanation has focused on Oman's membership in the nonaligned movement with the concluding of relations depicted as an attempt to balance East-West relations. Other considerations must include an Omani desire to ensure South Yemeni moderation; Qaboos has apparently made it clear to Moscow that improved relations are dependent on South Yemeni actions, on decreased aid from the United States, and on a belief by Qaboos that other GCC members were considering establishing relations with the Soviets and he did not want to be perceived as simply following the lead of the Saudis. Although Soviet presence in Muscat can be expected to increase in the future, for the time being Moscow has appointed a nonresident ambassador.

Relations with other states, both aligned and nonaligned, have been much less political and more economic. Relations with India and Pakistan, long Oman's major trading partners, remain close as both countries provide the bulk of the expatriate labor that keeps the Omani economy going. Japan, by virtue of its purchases on Omani oil and sale of automobiles and other consumer goods, is the sultanate's major trading partner and has been very active in the search for and development of new oil resources. West Germany, the home of former Prime Minister Tariq b. Taimur, has played a major role in construction, and Korea has helped to develop the country's fishing industry.

# 9

## Oman to 2000

Fifteen years of economic development and a young, popular ruler in Qaboos b. Sa'id portend a bright future for Oman, or so it would appear on the surface. However, the sultanate does face a number of possible difficulties that could disrupt its domestic stability or involve it in international conflict. Among the domestic problems facing the country are the matter of succession should Qaboos be removed from the scene, the long-term acceptability of the Al-Sa'id regime, the possible consequences of the country's ethnic divisions, and the economy. Internationally, the improved relations with South Yemen and the Soviet Union serve to alleviate tensions on Oman's southern border but also draw greater attention to the long-standing border disputes with GCC neighbors Saudi Arabia and the UAE.

### DOMESTIC AFFAIRS

Few would argue that Sultan Qaboos is in immediate danger of being toppled from power in Oman. His fifteen years as ruler have seen unprecedented economic growth, political reforms that have brought Omanis into the government and decision-making processes, a victory against communism in Dhofar, and the entry of Oman into the wider world. In sum, Qaboos has accumulated a great deal of popular support in the past decade and a half despite being a somewhat reclusive leader. That popularity, unlike the sultan's authority, is not absolute, however, and it could quickly dissipate. Economic benefits have been uneven, leading to dissatisfaction in interior Oman and growing concerns about corruption as the "Muscat Mafia" and a small number of British and even U.S. advisers seem to control the sultan. Religion, which is so closely tied to the traditional tribal order, is another area of concern: The Al-Sa'id regime is in violation of the Omani ideal of an elected, nonhereditary imamate and has long been in conflict with conservative supporters of a theocracy. Finally, there is the question of succession:

No provision has been made for a new ruler should Qaboos die suddenly or be somehow incapacitated.

### Cult and Corruption

Ten years ago in the flush of the victory in Dhofar and the rush of development projects in and around Muscat and Salalah, Qaboos was "Super Q" and no word was heard against him. There was tremendous optimism throughout the country that everyone would benefit from economic growth, despite concern about dwindling oil reserves. Occasionally someone would complain that a village lacked a school or clinic or perhaps wonder why a police station was always the first government building in a district, but these people were in the minority. Crowds would stand for hours after the police had closed the highway in anticipation of Qaboos' motorcade, joke about the inconvenience, and then surge forward and cheer when the black limousine surrounded by maroon-uniformed outriders on motocycles finally appeared. Those days are no more. By allowing a cult of personality to develop in which the success of the state is attributed personally to himself, Qaboos contributed to the erosion in his popularity. Problems, even natural disasters such as a recent drought, are now blamed on Qaboos.

This erosion has been exacerbated by the corruption of those around him. Corruption is a loaded word, especially in dealing with an Arab state, for our notions of conflict of interest and profiteering are very different. The Omanis consider it in no way corrupt for an individual to benefit himself and his family by using his official position. The money or contracts get spread widely, so almost everyone benefits. Unfortunately, several of Qaboos' advisers, especially those involved in the palace, development, and finance areas, have exceeded even Middle Eastern notions of corruption. Land holdings, government contracts, lucrative sponsorships—all are concentrated in the hands of four or five individuals whose blatant conspicuous consumption, such as the construction of ostentatious palaces along the airport highway at a time when many Omanis still lack even basic services, makes it more and more difficult for defenders of Qaboos to claim that the sultan is ignorant of what is going on.

If only Omanis were involved, criticism might not be so sharp, but Qaboos has continued the pattern begun by his father of surrounding himself with expatriate advisers. Although a great supporter of Omanization in the private sector and in government employment, the sultan seemingly does not have sufficient confidence in his own people to entrust them with control of intelligence and defense policy matters and sensitive areas of development, such as Ru'us al-Jibal. The apparent British and U.S. armlock on the sultan both discredits him with more nationalistic elements within Oman and provides the justification for support from outside the country to overthrow a puppet of Western imperialism.

### Religious and Tribal Concerns

Religious opposition is yet another cause for concern. Throughout its 240-year history, the Al-Sa'id regime has been at odds with the Omani tradition of an elected imamate. During the early years of Qaboos' reign, religious opposition was occasionally expressed, symbolically at least, by the flying of the white banner of the imamate over his new mosque in Nizwa or the ruins of Tanuf, a stronghold of imamate support during the 1957–1959 restoration movement. The popularity of Qaboos and the supposed diminishing of tribal allegiance and authority argued against any religious challenge to the regime, though. The sultan was also very supportive of religion, to deflect any potential criticism from that direction. The government built many new mosques, published religious works, supported an Islamic institute, and retained the sharia, and Qaboos maintains the appearance of being a devout Muslim. However, much of this religious activity has been in support of a generic kind of Islam rather than Ibadism. Mosque architecture is a good example; even though most new government mosques would be rather nondescript in Pakistan, they do not follow the traditional style of Ibadi mosques.

Declarations that tribal influence is no longer significant in Oman should not be taken seriously. The tribe is a 2,000-year-old institution that has shown remarkable staying power. Throughout Omani history tribal leaders have proved to be very pragmatic, sublimating their own power and authority when faced with superior power and/or authority. When there is a political vacuum, they reassert their positions. For an example of what could happen in Oman, one need only look to South Yemen where almost twenty years of scientific socialism have failed to destroy tribalism; the attempted coup of January 1986 quickly became a tribal struggle. Furthermore, the imamate is one institution that could galvanize both traditional and nationalist support because the imamate has traditionally been the focus of Omani nationalism is time of crisis, and its quasi-democratic principle of an elected, nonhereditary head of state is much more in line with modern theories of participatory democracy than is the anachronistic absolute monarchy of the Al-Sa'id. Much of the Qaboos' opposition to the introduction of democratic institutions can be attributed to the precedent that this would set vis-à-vis the legitimacy of his own position.

### Succession

Where concern over political stability and the imamate becomes especially acute is the matter of succession. Qaboos' position is secure, perhaps even among traditional leaders. There is some question as to whether that would be the case for Qaboos' successor—whoever that will be. Admittedly, this is a long-term issue because the sultan is only forty-six and in good health. He does not, however, have an heir. His 1975 marriage to Sayyid Tariq's daughter ended in divorce with no children, and Qaboos does not seem inclined to marry again. No provision for the succession has been announced publicly, although there is a reported agreement within the royal family that if the need arises, they will select a successor on the basis of consensus among themselves. It must be assumed, though, that other interests will have to be considered, and a struggle between the entrenched elite represented by the Muscat Mafia and more nationalistic, younger elites opposed to corruption in government should be anticipated.

The Al-Sa'id (the ruling branch of the large Al Bu Sa'id tribe) is a small family, numbering fewer than a hundred males (see Figure 9.1). A very small number are active in the government, and since the death of Sayyid Tariq, there is no dominant personality within the family. In the short term, five princes of Qaboos' generation, his uncles Fahr b. Taimur and Shabib b. Taimur, and cousins Thuwaini b. Shihab, Fahd b. Mahmud, and Faisal b. Ali, appear the most likely candidates to succeed. The younger generation of princes is led by Haitham b. Tariq. All are active in government.

### Ethnic Diversity

Another issue to be faced by Oman in the future is the country's ethnic diversity. Oman is a mosaic of religious and ethnic minorities that tend to be concentrated in specific regions of the country. The Al-Sa'id regime has traditionally been very liberal toward these minority groups with most complaints being that too much dependence was placed on resident Hindus, Shi'ites, or Baluchis to the exclusion of the Arab majority. That situation has begun to change markedly as Qaboos', or at least his government's, emphasis on Omanization has actually meant Arabization in practice. This result has alienated non-Arab minorities because discrimination is becoming much more evident as Liwatiyahs are denied promotion to senior government positions, Baluchis are forcibly resettled in isolated, poorly serviced new towns on the Batinah, Hindus are denied citizenship and harassed by government bureaucrats, or Zanzibaris have difficulties finding employment. Although these groups clearly do not threaten the stability of Oman, they can no longer be counted on to support the regime as absolutely as they once did.

Far more significant are groups like the Shihuh, with their tradition of independence and close proximity to the richer UAE, and the Dhofaris,

Figure 9.1   Al–Sa'id Royal Family

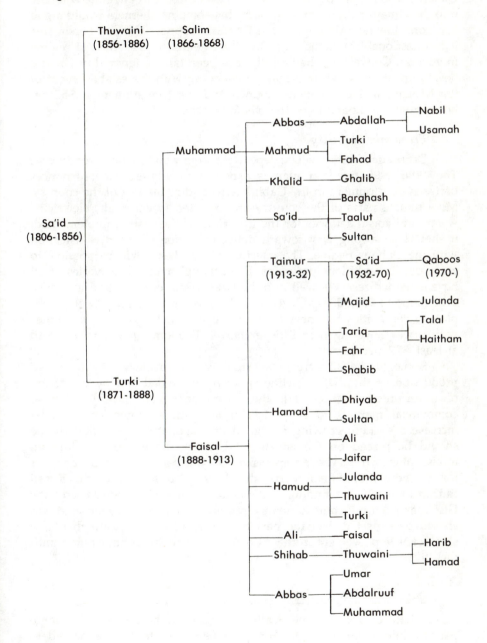

who are religiously and culturally distinct and have already proved their willingness to resort to violence if they feel that conditions demand it. Qaboos, who is part Dhofari, has made every effort to integrate Dhofaris into the Omani nation—an approach that some northerners would argue has gone too far. Although most Dhofaris support Qaboos personally, it is questionable whether that loyalty extends to the Al-Sa'id regime in general. Conversely, the Shihuh have been largely ignored in Oman's development, although that may be changing with the establishment of the Masandam Development Council and the formation of a Shihuhi home guard comparable to the Dhofari *firqat*.

### Economic Stability

Domestic stability will be dependent largely on economic conditions. The 1986–1990 five-year plan is expected to address the imbalances between development in the Capital Area and in the rest of the country. More remote parts of the country are expected to get roads, electricity, water, and social services for the first time. If the plan is implemented, it should go a long way toward deflecting some of the dissatisfaction with the Qaboos regime. The question is whether it will be possible to carry out its ambitious programs. Even though recent discoveries of oil have extended reserves well into the twenty-first century, and increased production to 500,000 bpd has enabled the second five-year development plan to reach its goals despite declining prices, the oil glut continues with prices hovering near $15 per barrel. Economic planners assumed at least $22 per barrel.

Some of the 30 percent shortfall can be made up by increased production as the PDO pipeline is slowly upgraded and by utilization of government reserves, but the government will have to turn to commercial markets to keep development on schedule and thereby increase a steadily growing foreign debt. Furthermore, not much hope should be placed on the efforts to diversify the economy. Although industrial growth has been impressive, OMC is expected to export copper for no more than fifteen years, the fledgling industries of the Rusail Industrial Estate are finding it difficult to sell their products, and the GCC has been reluctant to finance projects in Oman. Very slow growth should be expected over the next five years or at least until their is a significant improvement in the oil market, which is not anticipated until the 1990s.

### INTERNATIONAL AFFAIRS

Whatever occurs domestically in Oman will be influenced in large part by international events. Foreign affairs by late 1984 appeared to be more stable than at any other time in the recent history of the sultanate. The peace process with South Yemen was making good progress, the GCC heads of state had held a successful summit in Muscat, relations with the Soviet Union were established, the Tornado deal cemented the close relationship between Oman and Great Britain, and relations with the United States remained strong. Several months later the situation was not so clear.

### South Yemen

Events in South Yemen do not bode well for Oman. Muhammad Ali Nasser's attempt to eliminate hard-line Marxist opposition to his moderate domestic and foreign policies resulted only in his own overthrow and a muddled situation. Interim President al-Attas' letter to Qaboos assuring him that Aden wishes to continue its rapprochement offered immediate solace, but the situation in South Yemen still seems far from settled as the hard-liners in control seek to consolidate their grip on the country. Although the South Yemenis do not have the wherewithal to challenge Omani supremacy in Dhofar, a return to the pre-1982 policies would require greater Omani diligence on the border at a time when economic resources are already strained. Furthermore, the economic downturn might make the Omani people susceptible to Marxist propaganda, promising a more equitable distribution of wealth and political freedom no matter how false that propaganda might be.

### Gulf Neighbors

Relations between Oman and its Gulf neighbors are another area in which changes could occur over the next fifteen years. During the past fifteen years Qaboos has developed proper, if not friendly, relations with both Saudi Arabia and the UAE, primarily as a consequence of Oman's need for financial support and Saudi and UAE desire for a stable, conservative Oman. The GCC, with its goals of economic and defense coordination, has assisted this process. However, these public manifestations of solidarity should not obscure almost two centuries of distrust and conflict between the Al-Sa'id and the Saudis and various emirates, as demonstrated by Omani reluctance to participate in substantive economic and defense programs. Continued Omani participation in the GCC should not be assumed, especially if that organization continues to prove reluctant to finance projects in the sultanate.

A major issue is the border question. None of Oman's borders is demarked, and most are in dispute. The least controversial is that with Saudi Arabia through the Rub Al-Khali, but if Saudi claims were recognized, Omani oil fields would become part of the kingdom. The Omani government commissioned a study on this border in the early

1980s, apparently in preparation for discussions with the Saudis, but nothing has been done to date.

Far more serious are the various borders with the emirates both in Oman proper and with Ru'us al-Jibal. The status of these borders is much more complicated because the almost constant warfare of the nineteenth century and the shifting of tribal alliances make it nearly impossible to draw even a frontier. Furthermore, Dubai controls an enclave in Wadi Hatta, and Oman has an exclave on the Shimiliyah coast. The entire border between the emirates and Ru'us al-Jibal is disputed, and Oman and Ras al-Khaimah almost came to blows over the northeastern border in the late 1970s and early 1980s. That these are important issues to the parties involved is best demonstrated by the fact that crossing the border almost anywhere between Oman and the UAE can be a nightmare with a succession of immigration officials seemingly leapfrogging each other. It is no secret that Qaboos would like to see these issues resolved and that his preferred solution would have control of all of the Shimiliyah coast in Omani hands, thereby connecting Oman with Ru'us al-Jibal.

### Nonalignment

The long-term impact of the establishment of relations with the Soviet Union and the effect that will have on U.S.-Omani relations is difficult to judge. The Soviets have not opened an embassy in Muscat, although that should be expected to change. In fact, a Soviet presence in Muscat might prove especially fortuitous given the turn of events in Aden. It will be very difficult for the South Yemenis to take any action against Oman in the near term while their chief foreign backer is courting Qaboos. Certainly the entire move should not be seen as much more than the sultan's following his predictably unpredictable foreign policy that considers Oman's interests and prestige first and foremost. Relations with the Soviets are inevitable, and Qaboos does not wish to be caught following a Saudi lead.

Qaboos' comments about nonalignment to the contrary, Oman is still strongly allied to the West and will undoubtedly remain so. The visibility of the U.S. presence is appropriately low, except for the coterie of advisers of dubious backgrounds who surround the sultan, and the access agreement appears to be working satisfactorily for all concerned. Qaboos has been very cooperative in allowing limited access, as during the 1984 Kuwaiti plane highjacking to Tehran when U.S. planes landed at Masirah in preparation for a possible assault. Furthermore, in the matter of security, Qaboos has shown willingness to take the lead as the Saudis have subsequently negotiated access aggreements with the United States.

The concerns discussed here do, admittedly, represent worst cases. One should not assume that because these problems exist that Oman is likely to explode into chaos tomorrow or the next day or even next year. However, it is equally wrong and dangerous to assume that the sultanate is an idyllic, stable bastion of Western interest in the tempestuous Middle East region. Oman is a complex country with a rich history and culture, plagued by the same kind of ethnic divisions, fragile economy, weak political institutions of questionable legitimacy, difficulties with its neighbors, and uncertain relationships with the great powers that are so much a part of the Third World.

# Bibliographic Essay

Because of Oman's isolation, literature on the country before the 1970 coup is restricted to a few travelers' accounts, a limited number of scholarly studies based largely on British sources, and the memoirs of British officials who had served in Muscat. Since the coup and the opening up of the country, a great many books have appeared, ranging from the high-priced "coffee table" picture books to some outstanding monographs. Those interested in a fairly exhaustive bibliography on Oman should consult Joachim Duster and Fred Scholz's *Bibliography uber das Sultanat Oman* (Hamburg: Deutsches Orient-Institut, 1980) and the follow-up issues in *Oman Studies Bibliographic Information* (Tubingen: Centre for Documentation and Research on Oman and the Arabian Gulf, nos. 1–5, 1982–1983) (citations are in both German and English). A more limited, though more widely available, work is Frank Clements's *Oman* (Santa Barbara, Calif.: Clio Press, 1981). Recent publications are listed in both the *Middle East Journal* and the more thorough but not so widely available *Index Islamicus*.

No single volume survey of Oman exists. However, several general works on the Gulf region contain good discussions of the sultanate. One of the U.S. Army Area Handbooks by Richard F. Nyrop et al., *Persian Gulf States Country Studies* (Washington, D.C.: American University, 1984), is a good place to start and is especially strong on military affairs. David Long's *The Persian Gulf* (Boulder, Colo.: Westview Press, 1978) and Alvin Cottrell's *The Persian Gulf States* (Baltimore: Johns Hopkins University Press, 1980) are good introductions to Oman.

There are a number of outstanding studies of Oman's land and people. The best general work remains J. G. Lorimer's *Gazetteer of the Persian Gulf, 'Oman, and Central Arabia*, vol. 2 (Calcutta: Superintendent of Government Printing, 1908, with a 1970 reprint by Irish University Press), a work that can be misleading in its detail but is still valuable for information on places and people. John Duke Anthony's *Historical and Cultural Dictionary of the Sultanate of Oman and the Emirates of Eastern Arabia* (Metuchen, N.J.: Scarecrow Press, 1976) has a good description of the major regions and tribes of Oman. Probably the best narrative description of Omani geography and society is given in J. C. Wilkinson's *Water and Tribal Settlement in South-East Arabia* (Oxford: Clarendon Press, 1977). More recent specialized works on geography are limited and generally very technical, although N. L. Falcon's "The Masandam Expedition, 1971/1972," in the *Geographical Journal* (London), 139 (1973), pp. 1–19, is a good readable study of the physical geography of that remote region. Specialized works on flora and fauna include Don and Eloise Bosch and Kathleen Smythe's *Seashells of Oman* (London and New York: Longman, 1982); Michael Gallagher and Martin Woodcock's *The Birds of Oman* (London and New York: Quartet Books, 1980); J. Mandaville et al., *Scientific Results of the Flora and Fauna Survey of Oman* (Muscat: Ministry of Information and Culture, 1977).

The best survey of Ibadism remains T. Lewicki's "Ibadiyyah," in *Encyclopedia of Islam*, new edition, vol. 3 (Leiden and London: Brill, 1971), pp. 648–660. J. C. Wilkinson, in "The Ibadi Imama," in *Bulletin of the School of Oriental and African Studies* (London), 39 (1976), pp. 535–551, explains this distinctively Omani institution. J.R.L. Carter, in *Tribes in Oman* (London: Peninsular Publishing, 1982), provides an adequate discussion of tribes and tribalism in Oman and includes detailed genealogies of a number of tribes. Wilkinson's explanation of tribes in *Water and Tribal Settlement* is better. The Shihuh of Masandam have been described by Walter Dostal in "The Shihuh of Northern Oman," in the *Geographical Journal* (London), 138 (1972), pp. 1–7, and by Bertram Thomas in "The Kumzari Dialect of the Shihuh Tribe, Arabia, and a Vocabulary," in *Journal of the Royal Asiatic Society* (London), 4 (1930), pp. 785–854, and in "The Musandum Peninsula and its People, the Shihuh," in *Journal of the Royal Central Asian Society* (London), 16 (1929), pp. 71–86. Wendel Phillips's *Unknown Oman* (London: Longman, 1966) is the most detailed ethnographic and archeological study of Dhofar, although it must be used with care considering the author's lack of training and close personal and business relationship with ex-Sultan Sa'id. Dostal has also dealt with Dhofar in "Two South Arabian Tribes: al-Qara and al-Harasis," in *Arabian Studies* (London), 2 (1975), pp. 33–41, as has Thomas in "Four Strange Tongues from Central South Arabia, the Hadara Group," in *Proceedings of the British Academy* (London), 23 (1937), pp. 231–331. Readers with specialized interest in linguistics should consult Tom Johnstone's *Harsusi Lexicon* (London: Oxford University Press, 1977). Calvin H. Allen's "The Indian Merchant Community of Masqat," in *Bulletin of the School of Oriental and African Studies*

(London), 45 (1981), pp. 39–53, discusses the Hindu and Liwatiyah communities.

Traditional economic patterns of fishing, farming, and nomadism are discussed in J. C. Wilkinson's *Water and Tribal Settlement*, whereas more specialized accounts of Bedouin can be found in J. S. Birks's "The Shawawi Population of Northern Oman," in the *Journal of Oman Studies* (Muscat), 2 (1976), pp. 9–16, and Jorg Janzen's *Die Nomaden Dhofars* (Bamberg: Fach Geographie an der Universitat Bamberg, 1980). Omani agriculture is described in Paul Popenoe's "The Home of the Fardh Date," in *Monthly Bulletin of the State Commission of Horticulture* (Sacramento, Calif.), 3 (1914), pp. 9–19. J. S. Birks and Sally E. Letts, in "The Awamr," in the *Journal of Oman Studies* (Muscat), 2 (1976), pp. 93–100, describe the falaj specialists. The most detailed discussion of traditional fishing is provided by G.C.L. Bertram in *The Fisheries of Muscat and Oman* (Muscat: Director of Revenue, 1948). Traditional handicrafts are discussed in Ann and Daryl Hill and Norma Ashworth's *The Sultanate of Oman, a Heritage* (London and New York: Longman, 1977), with more detailed work on jewelry in Ruth Hawley's *Omani Silver* (New York and London: Longman, 1978). Carter's *Tribes in Oman* has an excellent discussion of handicrafts with some good photographs. Traditional seamanship is discussed in *Oman: A Seafaring Nation* (Muscat: Ministry of Information and Culture, 1979), whereas Tim Severin, *The Sindbad Voyage* (London: Hutchison, 1982) relates a ministry of national heritage–sponsored effort to adopt Sinbad the Sailor to Oman.

Serious archeological work began in Oman only after 1970, and no work before that time can be recommended. A first place to look for information on ancient Oman is the *Journal of Oman Studies*, the scholarly publication of the ministry of national heritage and culture edited by Paolo Costa. Much of the field work in the country has been published there, and though most of it makes dull reading for the nonspecialist, more general articles worthy of note are Maurizio Tosi's "The Dating of the Umm an-Nar Culture and the Proposed Sequence for Oman in the Third Millennium BC," in the *Journal of Oman Studies* (Muscat), 2 (1976), pp. 81–92, and Thiery Berthoud and Serge Cleuziou's "Farming Communities of the Oman Peninsula and the Copper of Makkan," in the *Journal of Oman Studies* (Muscat), 6 (1983), pp. 239–246, on Oman proper and A.F.L. Beeston's "The Settlement of Khor Rori," in the *Journal of Oman Studies* (Muscat), 2 (1976), pp. 39–42, on Dhofar. Another good article on the prehistoric period is Karen Frifelt's "Oman during the Third Millennium BC," in *South Asian Archaeology 1977*, vol. 1 (Naples: Instituto Universitario Orientale, 1979), pp. 567–587. Little research has been done on the period of the Persian occupation;

J. C. Wilkinson's *Water and Tribal Settlement* is the standard work on the period.

Much more material is available for the Islamic period. The principal Arabic source on Oman to early modern times is the *Kashf al-Juma'*, attributed to Sirhan b. Sa'id al-Izkawi, most of which is contained in Abdallah b. Humaid al-Salimi's *Tuhfat al-Ayan* (Cairo, 1928, and various reprints) and the much less reliable book by Humayd b. Ruzaik, *al-Fath al-Mubin* (Muscat, 1978), originally written in the mid–nineteenth century. Sections of the *Kashf* have been translated in E. C. Ross's *Annals of Oman* (Calcutta: Baptist Mission Press, 1874 reprinted by Oleander Press, Cambridge, 1984), and ibn Ruzaik is available in G. P. Badger's *History of the Imams and Seyyids of 'Oman* (London: Hakluyt Society, 1856 reprinted New York, Franklin, 1967), which contains a useful introduction surveying Omani history. General works covering the period, which are adequate but dated, include J. G. Lorimer's *Gazatteer*, S. B. Miles's (a British official in Muscat in the late nineteenth century) *Countries and Tribes of the Persian Gulf*, eds. 1 and 2 (London: Harrison, 1919; Frank Cass, 1966), and Wendell Phillips's *Oman* (New York: Reynal, 1967). A more specialized study of early Islam in Oman can be found in J. C. Wilkinson's *Water and Tribal Settlement* and his "The Julanda of Oman," in the *Journal of Oman Studies* (Muscat), 1 (1975), pp. 81–96, and "Bio-bibliographical Background to the Crisis Period in the Ibadi Imamate of Oman," in *Arabian Studies* (London), 3 (1976), pp. 137–64. On the rise of Sohar see Andrew Williamson's *Sohar and Omani Seafaring in the Indian Ocean* (Muscat: Petroleum Development Oman, 1973); J. C. Wilkinson's "Suhar in the Early Islamic Period," in *South Asian Archaeology 1977* (Naples: Instituto Universitario Orientale, 1979); and the various reports by Tony Wilkinson on his archaeological project in Sohar in the *Journal of Oman Studies*. J. C. Wilkinson's section, "Kalhat," in the *Encyclopaedia of Islam*, vol. 4, new edition, (Leiden and London: Brill, pp. 500–501), gives a brief account of that port's glory days. For Dhofar during this period see Paolo Costa's "The Study of the City of Zafar (al-Balid)," in the *Journal of Oman Studies* (Muscat), 5 (1979), pp. 111–50.

The Portuguese and Ya'aribah periods are very poorly documented; the above mentioned works of Lorimer, Miles, Badger, and Phillips are the most readily available. The Portuguese conquest is documented in Afonso de Alboquerque's *Commentaries of the Great Afonso de Alboquerque*, edited and translated by Walter de Gray (London: Hakluyt Society, 1875), and Muscat is mentioned briefly in other Portuguese chronicles. R. D. Bathurst's "Maritime Trade and Imamate Government: Two Principal Themes in the History of Oman to 1728," in Derek Hopwood, ed., *The Arabian Peninsula* (London: Allen and Unwin, 1972), pp. 89–106, is the best work available on the Ya'aribah, whereas two works by L. Lockhart, "The Menace of Muscat and its Consequences in the late Seventeenth and Early Eighteenth Centuries," in *Asiatic Review* (London), 42 (1946), pp. 363–369, and "Nadir Shah's Campaign in Oman, 1737–1744," in *Bulletin of the School of Oriental and African Studies* (London), 8 (1935), pp. 157–171, although dated, remain the standard works on the early eighteenth century. A new book by Patricia Risso, *Oman and Muscat, an Early Modern History* (New York: St. Martins, 1986) promises to fill this large gap in the literature on a most important period in Omani history.

The Al Bu Sa'id period is much better documented, especially because the British established a presence in Muscat and their representatives in the port sent a steady stream of information to Bombay. There is no single-volume survey of the period; three general essays, Rudolf Said-Reute's "The Al Bu Said Dynasty in Arabia and East Africa," in *Journal of the Royal Central Asian Society* (London), 16 (1929), pp. 417–432, and "Dates and References of the History of the Al Bu Sa'id Dynasty," in *Journal of the Royal Central Asian Society* (London), 18 (1931), pp. 233–255, and Bertram Thomas's "Arab Rule under the Al Bu Said Dynasty of Oman," in *Proceedings of the British Academy* (London), 24 (1938), pp. 27–53, are all dated. On Ahmad b. Sa'id, the founder of the dynasty, see Charles Beckingham's "The Reign of Ahmad ibn Said, Imam of Oman," in *Journal of the Royal Central Asian Society* (London), 28 (1941), pp. 257–260. Succeeding rulers are covered in C. H. Allen's "The State of Masqat in the Gulf and East Africa: 1785–1829," in *International Journal of Middle East Studies* (Los Angeles), 14 (1982), pp. 117–127. See also Carsten Niebuhr's *Travels through Arabia and Other Countries in the East* (Edinburgh, 1792) for an early traveler's account of Muscat.

Sa'id b. Sultan's long reign has been discussed in several books, including W. H. Ingrams's *Said b. Sultan* (Zanzibar, 1926), and Rudolf Said-Reute's, *Said b. Sultan, Ruler of Oman and Muscat* (London: Alexander Ousley, 1929). Vincenzo Maurizi's *History of Seyd Said* (London: John Booth, 1819, reprinted by Oleander Press, Cambridge, 1984) is an account of the author's activities in Muscat for three years to 1814; Wellsted's classic *Travels in Arabia* (London: J. Murray, 1838) gives a detailed first-hand account of interior Oman. Sa'id's activities in East Africa are discussed in detail in Reginald Coupland's *East Africa and Its Invaders from Earliest Times to the Death of Seyyid Said in 1856* (Oxford: Clarendon Press, 1938), and C. S. Nicholls's *The Swahili Coast* (London: Allen and Unwin, 1971). C. H. Allen is currently at work on a biography of Sayyid Sa'id. Oman in the late nineteenth century has been explained in the pioneering work by Robert Landen, *Oman Since 1856* (Princeton, N.J.: Princeton University Press, 1967), which is unfortunately out of print.

Valuable traveler's accounts for the period include several by the long-term British resident in Muscat Samuel Miles, "Across the Green Mountains of Oman," in *Geographical Journal* (London), 18 (1901), pp. 465–498, "Journal of an Excursion in Oman," in *Geographical Journal* (London), 7 (1896), pp. 522–537, "On the Border of the Great Desert," in *Geographical Journal* (London), 36 (1910), pp. 159–178, 405–425, and "On the Route between Sohar and Bereymi in Oman, with Note on the Zatt, or Gipsies, in Arabia," in *Journal of the Asiatic Society of Bengal* (Calcutta), 46 (1877), pp. 41–60; W. M. Pengally, "Remarks on a Portion of the Eastern Coast of Arabia between Muscat and Sohar," in *Transactions of the Bombay Geographical Society* (Bombay), 16 (1860–1862), pp. 30–39, and J. T. Bent, "Exploration of the Frankincense Country, Southern Arabia," in *Geographical Journal* (London), 6 (1895), pp. 109–134, on Dhofar.

An adequate survey of twentieth-century Oman is given by John Peterson in *Oman in the Twentieth Century* (New York and London: Barnes and Noble and Croom Helm, 1978). William Peyton's *Old Oman* (London: Stacey International, 1983) provides an excellent collection of historic photographs from the twentieth century. The principal Arabic account is Muhammad b. Abdallah al-Salimi's *Nahda al-Ayan* (Cairo, 1961), which continues his father's *Thufat* to the mid-1950s. Memoirs and travelers' accounts to World War II include Bertram Thomas's *Alarms and Excursions in Arabia* (Indianapolis: Bobbs-Merrill, 1931), and *Arabia Felix* (London: Reader's Union, 1938); Paul Harrison's (an American missionary doctor in Muscat early in the century) *Doctor in Arabia* (New York: John Day, 1940), and the classic by Wilfred Thesiger, *Arabian Sands* (New York: Dutton, 1959).

On the unification of Oman and subsequent civil war see the scholarly discussion of the issues in J. B. Kelly, *Sultanate and Imamate of Oman* (London: Oxford University Press, 1959); the memoirs of the commander of SAF David Smiley, *Arabian Assignment* (London: Cooper, 1975); the account of P. S. Allfree, a soldier, *Warlords of Oman* (London: Hale, 1967); and that of a journalist who accompanied Sa'id on his journey from Dhofar to Nizwah, James Morris, *Sultan in Oman* (London: Faber and Faber, 1957). On the late 1950s and early 1960s see the memoirs of Hugh Bousted, the director of development under Sa'id, *Wind in the Morning* (London: Chatto and Windus, 1971), and those of an oil company official, Ian Skeet, *Muscat and Oman* (London: Faber and Faber, 1974). By far the best available work on the coup and subsequent political and economic problems is John Townsend's *Oman*

(London: Croom and Helm, 1977). Townsend was an adviser to both Sa'id and Qaboos.

The Dhofar war has an extensive literature. Scholarly discussions of the insurgency include Fred Halliday's *Arabia without Sultans* (New York: Vintage, 1975), which gives a Marxist view; Howard Hensel's "Soviet Policy towards the Rebellion in Dhofar," in *Asian Affairs* (London), 69 (1982), pp. 183–207; John Peterson's "Guerrilla Warfare and Ideological Confrontation in the Arabian Peninsula: the Rebellion in Dhofar," in *World Affairs* (London), 139 (1977), pp. 67–92; and D. L. Price's article, "Oman: Insurgency and Development," in *Conflict Studies* (London), 53 (1975), pp. 3–19. Various participants in the conflict have also left accounts including John Akehurst's *We Won a War* (Salisbury, U.K.: Michael Russell, 1982); Ranulph Fiennes's *Where Soldiers Fear to Tread* (London: Hodder and Stoughton, 1975); and Tony Jeapes's *SAS: Operation Oman* (Nashville, Tenn.: Battery Press, 1980).

A large number of works on Oman since 1970 have been published although the quantity has not been matched by quality. For the general reader, Donald Hawley's *Oman and Its Renaissance* (London: Stacey International, 1977) and Michael Darlow and Richard Fawkes's *The Last Corner of Arabia* (London: Quartet Books, 1976) are recommended; Pauline Searle's *Dawn over Oman* (Beirut: Khayat, 1975), the Dutchess of St. Albans' *Where Time Stood Still* (London: Quartet Books, 1980), and Liesl Graz's *The Omanis: Sentinels of the Gulf* (London: Longman, 1982) are good; F. A. Clement's *Oman: the Reborn Land* (London and New York: Longman, 1980) has not been well received.

More scholarly works include a general survey by Fred Scholz, *Sultanate of Oman*, 2 vols. (Stuttgart: 1978–1979), C. H. Allen's article, "Oman and American Strategic Interests in the Arabian Gulf," in Robert Stookey, ed., *The Arabian Peninsula* (Stanford, Calif.: Hoover Institute, 1984), pp. 1–16, on domestic political issues; Anthony Cordesman's *The Gulf and the Search for Strategic Stability* (Boulder, Colo., and London: Westview Press and Mansell Publishing, 1984), on military affairs; and Dale Eickelman's article, "Kings and People: Oman's State Consultative Council," in *Middle East Journal* (Washington, D.C.), 38 (1984), pp. 51–71. On social change see J. C. Wilkinson's "Changes in the Structure of Village Life in Oman" in *Social and Economic Development in the Arab Gulf* (London: Croom Helm, 1980) and Fredrik Barth's *Sohar* (Baltimore and London: Johns Hopkins University Press, 1983). Excellent studies on women include the controversial one by Unni Wikan, *Behind the Veil in Arabia* (Baltimore and London, Johns Hopkins University Press, 1982) and Christine Eickelman's *Women and Community in Oman* (New York: New York University Press, 1984). Dale Eickelman is currently at work on a book on Omani politics.

Oman's relations with Britain have been discussed in several excellent works. J. B. Kelly's *Britain and the Persian Gulf 1795–1880* (Oxford: Clarendon Press, 1968) is the standard work on the nineteenth century and contains a wealth of general information on Omani history. B. C. Busch's *Britain and the Persian Gulf, 1894–1914* (Berkeley and Los Angeles: University of California Press, 1967) has the best discussions of Anglo-French relations in Oman. Texts of Oman's various international treaties can be found in C. U. Aitchison's *A Collection of Treaties, Engagements, and Sanads Relating to India and Neighboring Countries* (Delhi: Government of India, 1929–1933). Penelope Tuson's *The Records of the British Residency and Agencies in the Persian Gulf* (London: India Office Library and Records, 1979), a catalogue of the India Office Records, contains a useful discussion of British relations to 1948.

Omani relations with France are discussed in Anne Kroell's *Louis XIV, la Perse et Mascate* (Paris: Societe d'Histoire de l'Orient, 1977) and A. Auzoux's "La France et Muscate au XVIII et XIX Siecles," in *Revue d'Histoire Diplomatique* (Paris), 23 (1909), pp. 518–540, and 24 (1910), pp. 234–265. On U.S. relations see the document collection edited by J. D. Porter, *Oman and the Persian Gulf, 1835–1949* (Salisbury, N.C.: Documentary Publications, 1982) and Hermann Eilts's article "Ahmad b. Na'aman's Mission to the United States in 1840," in *Essex Institute Historical Collections* (Salem, Mass.), 106 (1970), pp. 219–277; as well as the interesting accounts by Americans in Muscat such as Edmund Roberts's *Embassy to the Eastern Courts of Cochin-China, Siam, and Muscat in the U.S. Sloop of War "Peacock," 1832–34* (New York: Harper Brothers, 1837, reprinted by Scholarly Resources, Wilmington, Del., 1972); W.S.W. Ruschenberger's *A Narrative of a Voyage Round the World, During the Years 1835, 36, and 37* (London: Bently, 1838, reprinted by Dawsons of Pall Mall, London, 1970); and J.B.F. Osgood, *Notes of Travel or Recollections of Majunga, Zanzibar, Muscat, Aden, Mocha, and other Eastern Ports* (Salem, Mass.: George Creamer, 1854, reprinted by Ayer, Frederick, Colo., 1972). Modern affairs are discussed in John Duke Anthony's *Oman, the Gulf and the United States* (Washington, D.C.: National Council on U.S.-Arab Relations, 1985). Zamil Muhammad al-Rashid's *Su'udi Relations with Eastern Arabia and Oman* (London: Luzac, 1981) is the best available discussion of that topic. More contemporary Omani foreign affairs are surveyed in Husain M. Albaharna's *The Arabian Gulf States*, 2nd ed. (Beirut: Librarie du Liban, 1975), and J. B. Kelly's *Eastern Arabian Frontiers* (London: Faber and Faber, 1964), which presents a pro-Abu Dhabi discussion of the Buraimi issue.

Keeping current on Oman is not an easy task because coverage in both the U.S. and British press is spotty. By far the best source of recent information is the weekly *Middle East Economic Digest* (*MEED*), although its expense limits its availability. The *Middle East Journal* publishes a brief chronology quarterly. *MEED* also publishes an annual special report on Oman, usually in November, which emphasizes economic affairs but contains a great deal of information. The Omani press is poorly developed and not easily accessable outside the country, but the National Day issue of the *Times of Oman* is interesting reading.

# Glossary of Foreign Words

**Barasti**  Palm frond houses found principally along the Batina coast

**Dhow**  Arab native ship

**Diwan**  Office of palace affairs

**Falaj/aflaj**  Omani irrigation systems

**Firqat**  The Dhofari home guard

**Ibadism**  Dominant sect of Islam in Oman, in which leadership is conferred on an elected imam

**Imam**  Elected spiritual and temporal head of the Ibadi sect of Islam

**Jabara**  Literally "tyrant," but used by Omani historians to describe leaders who are not properly elected imams

**Julanda**  Originally the title of the leader of the Arabs and later the name of the tribe that held that position

**Khanjar**  Curved dagger worn by most Omani males

**Majlis**  Public meetings commonly held by rulers (walis) throughout the Gulf region

**Mutawwi**  Tribespeople who actively support and fight for the imamate

**Qadi**  Judge in the Muslim court

**Qanat**  Underground irrigation channel

**Sails**  Alluvial outwash plains located at the mouths of wadis

**Sayyid**  General title of respect accorded to descendents of the prophet Muhammad but also used in Oman for members of the Al Bu Sa'id royal family

**Shaikh/sheikh**  The leader of a tribe

**Sharia**  Muslim law based on the Koran and traditions of the Prophet Muhammad

**Shi'ism**  Principal minority sect within Islam, it recognizes the authority of an hereditary imamate descendant from the Prophet Muhammad and allows the imam to interpret the sharia and to enact new law.

**Sunnism**  The majority denomination within Islam; it recognizes the authority of a caliph selected from the tribe of the Prophet Mu-

141

hammad whose religious authority is restricted to enforcing the sharia.

**Suq**   Marketplace

**Tamimah**   The paramount sheikh of a large or politically important tribe

**Ulema**   Literally "learned men"; used in reference to the class of religious scholars

**Wali**   Governor

**Wazir**   A government minister

**Wilayat**   Province or administrative subdivision

**Zakat**   The Muslim tax on agricultural produce

# Index

143

12 $^{6}$/98  13 $^{7}$/07